# THE
# *CIVIC*
# BRAND

# THE *CIVIC* BRAND

## The Power & Responsibility of Place

*by* RYAN SHORT

The MODassic Group
Salida, CO

Printed in the United States of America
First Printing: September 2025

ISBN 979-8-9994807-0-5  (hardcover)
ISBN 979-8-9994807-1-2 (paperback)
ISBN 979-8-9994807-2-9 (ebook)
ISBN 979-8-9994807-3-6 (audiobook)

Library of Congress Control Number: 2025916795

**For bulk purchases or to hire author Ryan Short to speak at your event, visit CivicBrand.com/book or email Hello@CivicBrand.com.**

To Banner, Andrew, and Charlie

# Contents

# Foreword

by Charles Marohn, founder of Strong Towns

In my work with cities, I've seen a familiar pattern: a place feels itself falling behind, so it reaches for something -- anything -- that might spark momentum. A bypass highway, a new industrial park, a national retail chain. If we just land this one employer, this one project, this one splashy win... then we'll be back on track.

For a moment, maybe that works. But more often, the result is a place that feels less like itself. More fragile, more dependent on outside forces, and more disconnected from the people who actually live there.

In The Civic Brand, Ryan Short tells us why. And, more importantly, he shows us what to do instead.

This book lays out a compelling argument: that what's missing from so many of our communities is not funding or planning or even leadership; it's a shared sense of identity. A story we tell ourselves and each other about who we are, what we value, and what kind of future we're building together. Not a slogan or a logo, but a brand in the truest sense: a vision that connects policy, design, investment, and culture.

That vision doesn't come from a focus group or a top-down campaign. It's uncovered -- patiently, through deep engagement -- and it belongs to everyone.

Ryan doesn't just advocate for branding as a technical exercise. He invites us to treat branding as stewardship. When done right, a civic brand becomes the connective tissue between people and place. It guides decisions. It strengthens civic pride. It allows local leaders -- elected, appointed, or informal -- to act with clarity and purpose, even in the face of short-term pressures.

And it helps us resist the temptation to imitate other places in the name of progress.

This idea -- that a place brand must be civic first, and not merely promotional -- is a crucial shift. We live in a time when places are being commodified and standardized at a breathtaking pace. Entire neighborhoods are being remade according to the latest trend or urbanist fad. This is often done at the expense of the very people who gave those places their culture and character.

In these civic transactions, we often witness "branding" used to cover up extraction, to sell something shiny on the surface while the substance erodes underneath.

This book is a reminder that we can do better. That we must do better.

The framework Ryan offers -- a triple bottom line of people, profit, and place -- is not just a moral argument, although it is that. It's also a practical one. Communities that center these three values are more resilient. They don't just chase growth; they guide it. They don't just market themselves to outsiders; they shape themselves in service of their people. And that, in turn, makes them more attractive, more stable, and more worth investing in. Financially, emotionally, across generations.

What I appreciate most about this book is that it doesn't flinch from complexity. Cities are messy. They're shaped by overlapping systems of governance, money, memory, and meaning. There's no simple fix. But there is a better way to work. And that better way starts with listening -- really listening -- to the people who make a place what it is. It starts with asking the right questions. And it starts with a commitment to design not for appearances, but for belonging.

Ryan writes about all of this with humility, clarity, and deep experience. He's been in the field, on the ground, in the workshops. He knows what it means to talk with real people, not just the loudest voices, but the quiet ones who rarely get asked. He's honest about the work it takes to build something lasting. He's not interested in easy wins. He's interested in getting it right.

If you're reading this book as a city leader, technical advisor, or someone who just cares a lot about their place, I encourage you to approach it not as a manual, but as an invitation. To rediscover what makes your place worth loving. To resist the pull toward sameness. To build something rooted and resilient.

You don't need to copy what someone else did. You don't need to wait for a savior or a slogan. You need to understand who you really are, in all its messiness and beauty, then bring your people along in shaping what comes next.

That's the promise of a civic brand. And that's the gift of this book.

- Charles Marohn
  Founder and President, Strong Towns

## Chapter 1: The *Civic* Brand

For much of the 20th century, we believed wildfires had to be fought at all costs, and therefore we focused efforts on ways to simply put fires out. Despite impressive advancements in firefighting, such as utilizing thermal imaging and the use of drones, it seems that wildfires, at least over the last thirty years, have become bigger, hotter, and more destructive. While we've gotten better at putting out individual fires, we've disrupted natural cycles, allowing fuel to accumulate and making wildfires even worse.

In many ways, our cities mirror this failure. We have more architects, engineers, data, and technology than ever before, and we have certainly gotten way better at doing very specific things that on their own are quite impressive. Yet many communities still suffer from unaffordable housing, gentrification, worsening climate impacts, overtourism, and cultural erosion, and countless municipalities are on the brink of a fiscal crisis.

Like forests that are more at risk from unmanaged undergrowth, our cities have become more at risk due to our fragmented efforts. The sum of our efforts and advancements somehow isn't adding up.

In the case of forests, it turns out the issue wasn't fire but how we've managed it. Indigenous cultures have long understood this and have been using fire to proactively manage forests for over ten thousand years. Just as we've fought fires without considering fire's role in a healthy ecosystem, we've tried to "fix" cities by reacting to problems and imposing short-term solutions rather than shaping a long-term, proactive vision. We've chased quick wins that end up making things worse in the long run.

A town with a struggling economy may offer incentives to recruit a large employer, make significant concessions to get a development project, or focus on increasing tourism. A community with declining civic pride may launch a marketing campaign to attempt to change the narrative only to realize the real issue is that people don't have a sense of ownership, making the effort feel hollow. A city facing traffic congestion keeps widening roads, thinking more lanes will ease the problem yet making the problem worse. These efforts may help in the short term but often lead to even greater challenges down the road.

Indigenous cultures didn't just react to fire. They managed it. The same must be true for cities. We can't just react to problems as they arise. We have to guide our places with intention.

For fire resilience to work, we can't rely solely on government agencies but instead must require everyday people to become active participants in shaping their environment. Property owners need to create defensible spaces, residents must support prescribed burns and be willing to fund fire departments, and developers and local businesses need to integrate fire-wise design.

The same is true for places. Communities can't just be managed from the top down. Healthy cities require civic pride and engagement from residents and local businesses. When people feel a strong connection to their place, they invest in it and care for it.

We need proactive and coordinated approaches to managing our communities. By simply reacting, our places have no real direction and are pushed and pulled in countless, uncoordinated directions, opening the door for the highest bidder, special interests, and outside entities to take control. That's when our communities start to lose their culture and identity and stop being proactive.

What is keeping our advances disjointed and reactive?

My answer: a brand.

Now, I understand that most people probably have branding pretty low on the list of things that matter for truly saving our places. It's typically thought of when it comes to selling something, marketing, and capitalist greed more than anything related to benefiting humanity.

I'm not talking about branding in a commercial or superficial sense but in its truest form, which is creating a shared identity and vision that guides all of our efforts. I'm also not talking about branding as an effort to lure outside investors or visitors to swoop in and save us either. That kind of desperation often leads to short-term thinking and extractive outcomes.

I'm talking about place branding that, when done right, becomes the connective tissue that gives communities a common direction that guides every new policy, project, and decision so that they add up to something bigger.

You may be thinking there are far more important ways to shape our places than branding. Perhaps you think urban design is the answer. You may think it's sustainability efforts, or you may think policy is the solution. But what is guiding that urban design? What guides the policy? Without a shared vision that connects all of those efforts, they will compete for attention and resources instead of working together. It's only when those things work together that they really have power. Place branding is what can provide that shared vision and the collective momentum needed to really make an impact. Housing, gentrification, revitalization, food insecurity, economic development, financial constraints, water shortages, walkability, parking, beautification, zoning, talent attraction, climate resilience - think about all of the big challenges that places are facing. It may not be obvious how place branding solves them directly, but I argue you can't even attempt to solve any of them without a strong place brand.

Even when we are doing the right things on individual issues, our solutions are often disconnected and lack the civic pride and buy-in needed to support them. They become divided, and we implement contradictory priorities. We simply react.

If you have a bad definition of "brand" or a bad experience with branding, then this may certainly sound farfetched. But with the proper definition of what a brand really is and what a place brand can be, there is nothing more powerful to draw people in, inspire, and serve as a guiding light and North Star that shapes and unites all downstream decisions and projects.

Brands can appear in a lot of forms. Most think of brands when it comes to companies and products, but sports teams, religions, and political movements are great examples for understanding the power of a brand. Some of these are things people devote their lives to, and in the case of religions and countries, some are even willing to die for them. On the surface, many may not consider these to even be brands, but that is absolutely what they are. They have a shared vision, shared language, and recognized symbols, and they bring people together to support and achieve that vision.

Cities can learn a lot from sports teams and how they build their brand and foster pride. The team colors are worn proudly, but it's not the team colors or mascot that people love and are attracted to. It's the shared experiences of sitting in the stands with your friends and celebrating a last-second victory, tailgating before the big game, or simply following your team through the ups and downs over the years. There is even camaraderie and connection in the losses.

Brands can be used for good, for evil, or simply to sell something. The best brands absolutely have an identity and visual symbols that, while they aren't the brand itself, serve as a reminder of the brand's vast depth and meaning. Religious symbols such as the cross for Christians, the Star of David in Judaism, and the crescent moon and star for Islam are basic symbols that on their own have no inherent meaning. However, over thousands of years, they have come to represent and remind their followers of a very deep meaning that evokes emotion and passion that guides and influences them on a daily basis. It takes the depths of their complex beliefs and long religious texts and gives them a simple way to communicate it and be reminded of it.

Brands have the power to represent deep and complex meaning in a quick and concise way, and the best brands serve as not just reminders of their past or what they are now but also as a guiding light for what they aspire to be.

Many think a brand is simply perception. That a place brand is the perception of a place and a consumer brand is the perception of that product or company. However, that is only half of the story. A true brand also moves a vision forward. It sits in between the current perception and its aspiration. That aspirational vision is what people are buying into and is what can serve as a filter for daily decision making. A company's brand should serve as a guide that shapes every decision it makes. The materials it uses, how it treats its employees, the impact it has. The same is true for a place brand.

Our places don't just need a symbol, colors, and messaging that remind us of the place. Instead, they desperately need that proactive vision that inspires its residents and drives its future through every decision that is made. Just like proactively managing a forest, we need to proactively manage our places. Let's not allow the power of branding to only be used by those that are trying to sell us something.

• • •

The past seventeen years of my career have been focused on branding and the power of place. My goal is to help every place rediscover their identity and develop an authentic shared vision and brand story that brings it to life and guides it to a prosperous future. I intentionally used the word "rediscover," and we almost never use the term "rebranding." That is because we believe places already have a brand, but it hasn't been clearly defined or perhaps lies in potential. A business can rebrand on a whim and simply choose to go in an entirely new direction to chase a market trend or strategic advantage, but places are different. They are complex, living systems with a history and are controlled by so many different entities that they can't, and in most cases shouldn't, radically change directions. A community often needs to come together and rediscover its brand. When this is done correctly, it can inspire civic pride and benefit locals while still attracting those outside visitors and investment, all in a way that works for the community.

One of the most important reasons to take on a place branding project is not to simply attract growth but instead to get ahead of the growth and ensure that it is the right kind of growth for your community, just like we have to get ahead of fire to properly manage our forests. It's more about defining and protecting your identity and ensuring that as you grow and attract visitors and investment, you stay true to what your community values. While some cities and areas of the country are in a state of decline, others are radically growing whether they want to or not. Therefore, establishing a strong place brand is vital to both reverse that decline as well as to get ahead of the growth and avoid letting growth simply happen to you.

• • •

When my wife and I started our company, we didn't initially set out to be a city and place branding agency. Instead, we worked with a wide range of companies, and what we were really good at was user experience. When most people use the term user experience or UX, they are likely talking about the design of digital interfaces and things like apps and websites. Our firm did a fair amount of web design, and we were definitely thinking a lot about how users used digital tools. However, we were very brand focused, so we thought a lot more broadly than just how a user uses a website. We thought about their entire consumer journey. I'm a big believer in and student of the human-centered design approach, which takes elements of user experience, research, and iteration and applies that in a framework to help you constantly improve designs and processes. Human-centered design is relevant to understanding how someone uses anything, whether it's a product, a website, a door, or how they experience their community. It is about deeply understanding users and what their goals are, recognizing where they struggle, and then designing and iterating to improve their experience.

One of my favorite books is *The Design of Everyday Things* by Don Norman. In his book, he makes the point that when someone struggles to understand how to use something, it's very likely not the fault of the user but rather the designer. An example of this is "Norman doors," which have been named after him. A Norman door is what you call those super annoying doors that are unclear whether you should push or pull and leave you feeling embarrassed when you pull on a door that needs to be pushed. Don Norman's book is about putting the responsibility on the designer to truly understand their audience and the user. This approach to design applies not just to how we should design doors but to how we should approach the design of everything from websites to buildings, sidewalks, and cities.

As we got better and better at that, our firm started to make our shift into working exclusively with cities and places. We realized that our process of user experience and human-centered design was just a better way to do public engagement and that our places were the most meaningful thing we could use our talents and careers to try to improve. Cities and planning firms had been doing public engagement for a long time, but to be honest, we very quickly saw that most were doing a really poor job of it. At their best, they were informing the public, and at their worst, they were completely ignoring and disenfranchising entire segments of the population while only catering to the louder and easier-to-reach segments of the population. We set out to change that.

This is a book about "place," and I think it's a requirement that you can't write a book about place without mentioning Jane Jacobs. Jane was an activist in New York City. In the urban planning world, she's a bit of a legend. Jane's book, *The Death and Life of Great*

*American Cities*, really changed the game for how many think about and approach building cities and who we are designing for.

We saw a strong connection between how we thought about designing for people and how Jane thought about creating places for people. Recognizing the importance of public engagement and place and that most cities weren't getting it right, we latched on to a famous quote of hers and used it as the mission of our company: "Cities have the capability of providing something for everybody, only because, and only when, they are created by everybody." This serves as our mission statement, and we start every place-branding project with public engagement. We deeply engage the locals to understand their needs and challenges before we start thinking about external audiences.

• • •

While CivicBrand is the name of our company, this book isn't about us. Instead, I am making the case for an intentional focus on how we shape our places and how place branding, when done right, is the very necessary yet often missing link that pulls everything together. My term for a place brand done right is a *civic* brand.

A *civic* brand is rooted in public engagement and guided by a triple bottom line of people, profit, and planet. There are a lot of place brands that purely focus on growth or tourism and end up harming their local communities. Those are still place brands but they aren't good place brands, so to me, they aren't *civic* brands.

A triple bottom line simply means that you don't judge success by profit alone. You also consider the impact on its people and the planet. Instead of one bottom line of just profit, there are three equal bottom lines: people, profit, and the planet. I'm a big believer in this approach for businesses and an even bigger believer in this approach when it comes to place branding.

The one tweak I like to make in the triple bottom line approach when applying it to place branding is to broaden the planet category and use the term "place" instead. While that may seem less broad at first, I argue it's even broader. While the term planet speaks to the environmental aspects, which are vital and should be considered in a triple bottom line analysis of a place brand, the term "place" still captures the environmental aspects as our planet is our ultimate place. However, it also makes us consider how a place brand impacts our built environment and those physical aspects of our places that impact our health, happiness, and civic pride.

You can have an impressive place brand that can win awards, fill up hotels, and drive economic growth. Would that be a success? Perhaps...if that's your only measure of success. My belief is that places need to take a more holistic approach to the impacts of place and take greater responsibility for how we shape, manage, and measure the success of our places.

In this book, I share stories and many lessons learned with the hope of inspiring you so that more places can become the best versions of themselves. Our places are the sum of everything in them. Every individual and every business make their own contribution in their own way, and only when we zoom out does it then come together as a singular place.

The same is true of the movement around place as it takes a lot of different voices, perspectives, and contributions to really make an impact. This book is hopefully just one more voice in the ongoing movement that champions people and place. In this book, I reference many others who are all chipping away at similar challenges but from their own angles and disciplines. Some through a fiscal lens and others through urban design, psychology, health, activism, or business. I strongly believe that a place brand is often the missing link that is desperately needed to connect all of these other efforts. Without that inspiring and proactive shared vision, we are just putting out small fires and operating in silos. Our communities deserve to be guided by purpose. This book is a call to rediscover the power of place branding and to build places we are proud to call home.

The following statements form a manifesto of what a *civic* brand is and why it matters. Each statement appears later in the book where it anchors key ideas collectively defining a *civic* brand:

- A *civic* brand embraces how place shapes us and we shape it.

- A *civic* brand strengthens our sense of ownership.

- A *civic* brand is the North Star that guides design, policy, and culture.

- A *civic* brand leads with clarity and intention.

- A *civic* brand doesn't imitate culture, it reflects and serves it.

- A *civic* brand is not a campaign, it's a commitment.

- A *civic* brand balances people, profit, and place.

- A *civic* brand is shaped by everyone and owned by no one.

- A *civic* brand guides growth to serve locals.

- A *civic* brand is uncovered, not invented.

- A *civic* brand connects diverse voices through shared values.

- A *civic* brand embraces tension as a tool, not a threat.

- A *civic* brand makes engagement a culture, not a task.

- A *civic* brand meets people where they are.

- A *civic* brand values viewpoints over voting.

- A *civic* brand listens before it leads.

- A *civic* brand turns insight into action.

- A *civic* brand unites every project around a shared purpose.

- A *civic* brand reflects authenticity and aspiration.

- A *civic* brand creates a shared language.

- A *civic* brand shows up in everyday decisions.

- A *civic* brand helps people share what they love.

- A *civic* brand is shaped through shared stewardship.

- A *civic* brand proves its value through action.

# PART I: THE POWER OF PLACE

## Chapter 2: Why Place Matters

The places we inhabit are perhaps the most important factor that impacts our lives. Our places can be inspiring and provide us with opportunity, or they can be draining and damage our well-being. They are the foundation of our daily experiences and the backdrop to our lives, yet no single entity, organization, or government fully control them. That is both the beauty and complexity of place. If we value our places that have such a huge impact on us, and if we want to have a positive and lasting impact on them, we must first understand how they shape us and how we shape them.

What is a "place" and why that word? On the one hand, the word "place" is all-encompassing. It's a nice, short word that can apply to a neighborhood, a city, a county, a region, or even our planet. It's an easy term that we all recognize that captures all of those things. "Place" also captures more than just a location. There's something special about the term "place."

A place certainly has physical characteristics and is often identified by its boundaries, landmarks, architecture, and geography. However, what makes the term "place" special is that it captures more than just the physical elements. It also captures the cultural elements, such as traditions, stories, experiences, and history.

It also captures intangible characteristics and emotions, like the coziness of your favorite coffee shop or the way it feels to stroll down a historic main street. A place can hold and influence memories, such as the park you played at as a child or the mural that was a backdrop to a treasured photo. All of these examples speak to something very different than just the physical location. It starts to capture feelings and emotions and things that can't just be viewed on a map.

Many cities conduct historical surveys. Not to be confused with the type of surveys where you're asking people questions, this type of survey is instead a historical analysis and documentation of all the buildings and architecture of historical significance in a city. These surveys help a city know what historical assets it has so that it can ultimately protect them. However, the best surveys go beyond just documenting the physical buildings and instead seek to understand the stories within those buildings, the role they played, and how they impacted the people at that time.

This level of survey is important so that cities know what assets they have and can protect them through historical designations and protections. While these surveys always document a building's age, architectural style, and construction materials, that information alone doesn't fully capture the significance of the place. Protecting physical assets without understanding their cultural and historical significance reduces a city's history to a checklist of aesthetics and real estate. Connecting both the tangible and intangible is what makes a place unique and irreplaceable.

Derek Avery, a small-scale developer, shared a powerful example of this when he came on our podcast, *Eyes On The Street*. During a construction project in Houston's Fourth Ward, a contractor unknowingly threw away bricks from a historic brick street. It turned out these bricks had been laid by freed slaves in the 1800s. To the contractor, they were just old bricks, but to the community, these bricks carried deep cultural significance representing a tangible connection to the past. This is a powerful example of why preserving the stories behind our places is just as important as preserving the physical assets. This wasn't just a loss of old bricks. It was a loss of history and identity.

So place, I think, is a great term because it seeks to understand everything that contributes to its "sense of place." That's a phrase that we've all heard, and it speaks to the summation of everything about a place including both the physical and experiential.

The places we inhabit are all-encompassing and shape us all in more ways than we realize. It's like water for fish. If the water is bad, it doesn't matter what else happens. The fish will not be healthy.

Think about the experience of an average commuter living alone in a large, sprawling city. They wake up and go to their car, which is in an attached garage. They get in their car, and they make their twenty- to forty-minute commute alone to work. They get to their office, park in a parking garage, go to their office, find their way to their desk, do their work, and then get back in their car and make the commute back home. While that is certainly over-simplified, I don't think it's too uncommon of an experience for many. In this scenario, that person is completely insulated by their place. They almost never have to actually go outside. They go from air-conditioned space to air-conditioned space, so they're not even engaging with the outdoors and weather. They're often alone. They are alone as they drive their car, and while they may work with others, they are likely alone at their computer for the majority of the day. Their place is insulating them from both people and the environment.

If this scenario is a reality for millions of people, it's no wonder we have increasing levels of unhappiness, decreasing health, and increased divisiveness. The way people interact with their surroundings directly impacts their well-being as well as their sense of responsibility toward their community. In this context, not only is the place negatively impacting the individual through isolation, physical inactivity, and a lack of connection but that individual is likely, in turn, unintentionally negatively impacting their place. When people don't engage with their community, they lack the pride and sense of responsibility that they would otherwise have if they were more immersed. They may pass by streets and parks in their car without noticing or caring about their upkeep. With no connection to the outdoors, they're more likely to feel indifferent to environmental concerns, such as how pollution or sprawl are impacting their community. This cycle of disengagement creates a feedback loop where both the individual and the place suffer. Charles Montgomery, author of *Happy City*, does a great job in his book of illustrating how urban design and city planning directly shape our happiness. I highly recommend reading it if you haven't already.

On the contrary, place can greatly benefit you and, in turn, encourage you to positively impact it. If your neighborhood is more walkable, it may encourage you to get outside and engage with neighbors and even strangers. If you're active, walking, engaging with people, and experiencing the outdoors, you're also going to be more aware of problems and changes. You'll notice trash by the curb that you'd miss if you passed by at fifty miles an hour in a car. You're more likely to notice if the neighbor you pass each day seems a little down one day. You'll notice if it's hotter than normal or if there is smoke in the air. Over time those things may move you to act. It may cause you to pick up some trash, make you stop and talk to that person and ask how they are doing, and make you more aware of climate and environmental threats. As I was writing this chapter, I came across a LinkedIn post by Dr. Vivek Murthy, who was the Surgeon General of the United States. As he was leaving office, he posted a document titled "My Parting Prescription for America." His ultimate prescription for us all was to "choose community." He recognized that community and places with unique identities where diverse people can come together and contribute their different perspectives doesn't just make our lives better. It literally makes us healthier.

Ann Sussman, the author of *Cognitive Architecture*, does a brilliant job of explaining how the design and architecture of buildings impact our emotions and well-being. Her work explores how our brains are impacted by architecture and how we are hardwired to react to our surroundings. We are all shaping our places, and at the same time, our places are shaping us back.

This is confirmed over and over by people much smarter than me, and while the neuroscience behind it may be a bit over my head, what makes it real for me is when I learn these same lessons through my experience in nature and the outdoors. Picture a river flowing through a canyon. That river has been carving out and forming that canyon for millions of years. As the water flows and tumbles over rocks, it slowly carves and sweeps away layers of sand and rock, layer by layer, and over time starts to form that canyon. But at the same time, the canyon is shaping the path of the river. The river is held within the canyon. It's bound and constrained by the walls of the canyon controlling and shaping where the water can go. The river is shaping the canyon, and the canyon is shaping the river. We are shaping our built environment, and in turn, our built environment is shaping us.

## A *civic* brand embraces how place shapes us and we shape it.

When someone engages with their place, they are more likely to have pride in it. When they have pride in it, they are more likely to want to protect it. They want it to be the best version that it can be. And when a lot of people all have civic pride in the same place, there is nothing more powerful. Those are the places where things are happening. Those are the places that are resilient and moving forward. When you have civic pride, so much can be done to shape a place for good. Our places can contribute civic pride or detract from civic pride, and people in that community can contribute to civic pride or detract from civic pride through their actions.

• • •

A key ingredient of civic pride is ownership. Not just in the literal sense of owning property or a business but also in the broader sense of feeling like you have a stake in your place. When people have a sense of ownership, they care for things differently. They show up, participate, and are more actively involved in shaping their communities.

This sense of ownership doesn't require homeownership or business ownership, but these do play a role. When a neighborhood is full of locally owned businesses, decisions are made by people that live in that community. They tend to care more about the community's future. Decades ago, your local hardware store, pharmacy, and diner were likely owned by someone in your community, and they likely were more invested in the town and built personal relationships with their customers. Today most of those businesses are owned by national chains, where decisions are made in corporate boardrooms far away and profits flow out of the community rather than staying in it.

This shift in ownership impacts not just economics but identity and connection. When fewer people have the ability to own businesses or homes in their community, there's a risk of detachment and the community losing its identity. If people feel like they have no long-term stake, their sense of ownership erodes. A place can start to feel temporary rather than like something worth fighting for.

What's happening at the local business level mirrors a larger trend across society, where ownership is becoming less common, not by accident but by design. Companies have figured out that it's more profitable to keep people paying for something indefinitely versus them owning it outright. Today most of what we use is rented, subscribed to, or designed to be replaced.

Computer software is a great example. Back when we first started our company and we needed Adobe Creative Suite, we made a one-time purchase and owned it. We could use it as much as we wanted to and wouldn't need to pay again until we decided we wanted to upgrade to their new version. It wasn't cheap, but we owned it. Today Adobe is a subscription service, where they charge a monthly fee for eternity. The same goes for music, movies, and even our phones. Today most people don't own their phones outright. They simply make monthly payments and trade in their old phone every couple of years for the latest model, and they never stop paying. In fact, the Netflix documentary, *Buy Now! The Shopping Conspiracy,* estimates that globally, thirteen million phones are thrown away every single day. Whether it's streaming services, cloud storage, or car leases, ownership is on the decline. We don't own as many things anymore, and fewer things are designed to really last. Products are more temporary, yet we'll eternally pay for them. And as long as we have the latest phone, the latest content, and the latest gadget, most don't seem to mind.

This isn't just impacting technology and consumer products. It's a systemic shift that's impacting our places. A town where most businesses are locally owned feels very different from a town that is full of national chains. A neighborhood with higher rates of homeownership often sees more long-term stability than one full of rentals, but don't let that make you think it's because renters are any less important to their community. In fact, renters play a critical role in shaping the identity and culture of a place. Many of your artists, service industry workers, and young adults are often renters, and they are some of the biggest drivers of culture and identity. The real challenge isn't that they rent, but that without at least the ability to have ownership, they have less control over their future in that community. When housing costs rise, renters that have helped define a place's character face the risk of being displaced and unable to stay in the very neighborhoods they helped shape. Simply having access to ownership and a culture of entrepreneurial investment is essential to civic pride. When those things go away, communities struggle.

• • •

Historically, many communities were built around a single industry or employer, and the company provided not just jobs but a sense of stability and identity to the community. Over generations, more and more people became reliant on that employer and, in doing so, unknowingly gave up something vital.

In Two Rivers, Wisconsin, Hamilton Manufacturing Company shaped the town for more than a century. Founded in the late 1800s, Hamilton eventually grew into the largest manufacturer of wood type in the country. It produced nearly all of the wood type used to print newspapers, posters, and advertisements in the United States. As Hamilton grew, so did the town's reliance on it.

For generations, the people of Two Rivers didn't need to think about entrepreneurship or diversification as the company provided stability. While the town was once entrepreneurial, leading to the growth of Hamilton, over time it lost that entrepreneurial spirit. Hamilton was the economic backbone of the town, and as a result, the community became dependent on it. When the company eventually shut down, it left a void bigger than just the lost jobs. The town realized it had lost not just its main employer but it had also lost its entrepreneurial spirit along the way. Many residents believed the only path forward was for another large employer to come in and take Hamilton's place rather than locals creating something new from within.

That is, until a new generation started to step up and rediscover what ownership really meant. We were fortunate to work with Two Rivers, Wisconsin, on a place-branding strategy to help them find this new path forward. During our engagement process, one of the standout people we had the chance to meet was Emilee Rysticken.

Emilee didn't wait for a large employer to return. At just seventeen years old, she started her own business, Scream 'N Conuts, an ice cream shop that she dreamed up while on an overseas trip. Rather than leaving town like so many of her peers, she rolled up her sleeves, renovated an old building, and started her business. When others questioned why she would start a business in what they saw as a "dying town," she ignored them as she saw potential. She wasn't focused on what Two Rivers had lost and what it used to be. She was focused on what it could be. Ironically, Two Rivers is also where the ice cream sundae was invented, so Emilee is naturally embracing the entrepreneurial spirit and identity that originally founded Two Rivers. She's now a leader in shaping the next era of the town.

## A *civic* brand strengthens our sense of ownership.

Emilee's story is a reminder that places thrive when people feel a sense of ownership and believe they have the power to shape and improve them. Hamilton has closed, and all that remains is the Hamilton Wood Type Museum, which is an amazing place and a must-visit. Our team was able to tour the museum and even create custom wood type letterpress posters promoting the public workshop that we held as part of the branding process. While the museum remains and is a very nice nod to the town's past and design legacy in the United States, it is young entrepreneurs like Emilee who are shaping the future of Two Rivers. Her shop is more than just a place to buy ice cream. It sends a signal of optimism that the community doesn't need to wait around for outside investment to be revitalized.

A strong sense of ownership, whether actual ownership of property or a feeling of ownership, is what makes the difference between places that thrive and those that fail. Places succeed when people believe they have the power to make a difference. If we want to create places that people love, we must start by making sure people have a sense of ownership and know they can make a difference.

• • •

Everyone deserves to love where they live and feel a sense of civic pride. Place branding isn't just for the top tourism destinations or cities on Top 10 lists of best places to live. Our industry is plagued by silly city rankings and Top 10 lists. The reality is there are a lot of people and a lot of places, and most places just need to be good places that people can love and be proud of.

Someone may live in a town that nobody would consider visiting on vacation, but that doesn't mean that they shouldn't take pride in it and don't deserve to love where they live.

When we think about place branding, the goal isn't to turn every place into a tourist hot spot. Instead, the goal is to help every place become a better version of itself by strengthening its unique character, improving the quality of life, and increasing opportunity for the people that call it home.

While I believe in many urbanist principles, this isn't yet another urbanist book that's here to say suburbs are evil and insist every place must become a hip, walkable downtown. Suburbs, just like all places, have opportunities to improve in ways that can enhance their residents' lives. The goal isn't to say that one place is better than another. The goal is simply to make every place better for the people that are already there.

There are certainly challenges with suburban development, but plenty of others have already written extensively on that topic. Instead, I want to focus on how, through a triple bottom line approach to place branding, we can help all places evolve and become places that are more financially stable and are better for both people and the environment. That doesn't mean turning them into something they're not. It simply means identifying opportunities for improvement, enhancing community connections, fostering a stronger sense of place, and making smarter, more sustainable choices that are driven by their unique goals and identity so they can become stronger, healthier, and more lovable.

Whether we are doing work on engagement, place branding, or placemaking, our focus is simply, how can this place become the best version of itself? How can it help people be happier, be healthier, and have more opportunity while creating more civic pride? Once you help people have more civic pride, they are now armed with the ability to start positively impacting their place. Like the river, they are no longer just shaped by the canyon walls. They have become the powerful water that is shaping the canyon.

# Chapter 3: The Case for Place Branding

Our places shape every aspect of our lives, and there are some really pressing issues and challenges that our places and our planet, the ultimate place, are facing. We stand no chance of saving the planet without collective action from everyone and until we start saving our individual neighborhoods, towns, and cities first.

I firmly believe that place branding, when done correctly, can be the most powerful way to do that. As I stated in the introduction, many people probably rank branding pretty low on the list of things that truly matter for humanity. It is often seen as a tool just for selling something and too often gets confused with marketing and advertising more than anything making a positive impact in our world.

A *civic* brand can create a shared sense of purpose and pride and the collective momentum that is needed to take on the big challenges that our places face. To take on these big challenges, we don't just need more place brands. We need more *civic* brands.

## A *civic* brand is the North Star that guides design, policy, and culture.

In High Point, North Carolina, the branding and placemaking work we led has helped that community address food insecurities, housing challenges, and reinvestment in downtown, not because the brand magically solved these problems directly but because the brand served as that North Star. It was the catalyst that created a shared vision, prioritized and aligned projects, and showed residents their role in shaping the community. It empowered them and identified the areas that needed to be addressed to achieve their vision.

All the big challenges places are facing - housing, gentrification, revitalization, food insecurity, economic development, overtourism, walkability, parking, beautification, zoning, talent attraction, budget deficits - aren't solved directly by a place brand, but you can't solve any of them without a place brand.

This is why cities often feel like they are being pulled in a million different directions and are being reactive and simply putting out fires. They may be doing the right things, but they haven't figured out how they all fit together.

To further make the case for place branding and show you that this is a priority that every community should pay attention to, I want to present the identity case, the ethical case, the economic case, and the strategic case for place branding.

**The Identity Case**

More than ever, places are losing their identity. Decreasing ownership, globalization, and the way we have built cities in the post-war era all contribute to this. A lot has been written and studied about the devastating effects of how freeways were built that ripped right through the heart of many communities. For decades, bad design, including strip centers and soulless master-planned developments with faux facades and cheap construction, have created an uninspired and homogenized landscape. While the negative impacts of bad design are fairly obvious, I think what is interesting to consider is how even "good design" has hurt our communities. While more communities than ever have actively focused on improving their identities, I think many have unintentionally whitewashed their true identity in the process by following global design trends.

More and more people are recognizing that aesthetics matter and that good design is important. The rise of platforms like Instagram, Pinterest, Etsy, user-friendly creative tools, interior design TV shows, and affordable good design like IKEA have democratized access to good design, and the general public's appreciation and recognition of good design has never been higher.

As good design trends spread via the internet, we are seeing more and more places and more and more things look the same. It may look on trend, it may look good, but it all looks the same.

Coffee shops, hotels, architecture, urban design, automobile design, fashion, logo design, and typography are all merging in the middle. The good news is that businesses can quickly and easily fire up a website, create a logo, and design their storefront without any design skills or design professionals and it'll probably look good and on trend, assuming they have a decent eye. But looking good in businesses is one small piece of the puzzle. How do they compete? How are they different, and how are they positioned against their competitors? If they look good but they look the same as all their competitors, how do they stand out? If it's easy for them to apply these generic good design aesthetics, then it's also easy for their competitors to apply the same good design aesthetics.

So one new coffee shop looks like the next, whether it's down the street, in the next town over, or in another country.

In 2016, Kyle Chayka coined the term "AirSpace" in an article for *The Verge*, and I probably haven't stopped thinking about it since.

In the article, he describes the AirSpace aesthetic as:

> The realm of coffee shops, bars, startup offices, and co-live/work spaces that share the same hallmarks everywhere you go: a profusion of symbols of comfort and quality, at least to a certain connoisseurial mindset. Minimalist furniture. Craft beer and avocado toast. Reclaimed wood. Industrial lighting. Cortados. Fast internet. The homogeneity of these spaces means that traveling between them is frictionless. Changing places can be as painless as reloading a website. You might not even realize you're not where you started.

And here's the thing: minimalist furniture, craft beer, Edison bulbs - I like all those things! We can all picture a coffee shop or coworking space that has that aesthetic, and we probably like it.

If I lived in a town with a struggling downtown, I'd want a well-designed coffee shop to come in and spruce up a vacant storefront. It would likely do really well, and it would spur development for the rest of the town. Who wouldn't want their town to feel more vibrant and modern? Everyone deserves to have well-designed things in their town, in their home, and at their businesses.

If we aren't careful, every coffee shop, every Main Street, every business, and every town will end up looking the same. There would be no reason to travel and no reason to explore, because you'd find the same aesthetic everywhere. While some may argue that's a good thing, it sounds like a miserable existence to me. I know that I'm guilty of walking into a coffee shop in a town I've never been to and thinking, *Wow, this place is cool,* even though it looks exactly like the cool coffee shop in my town. So I get that it's not immediately obvious how this is a problem.

The term AirSpace came from studying how the interior design aesthetic of Airbnbs around the world is becoming the same. When Airbnb was first launched, its whole pitch was "Live like a local," a tagline that I loved as you weren't just booking a hotel and being an average tourist but instead were stepping into a real person's home and experiencing their town the way locals did.

Unfortunately, as Airbnb became more successful and short-term rentals became an entire industry of its own, people started to realize that certain interior design aesthetics performed better on the platform and were booked more often and at higher rates. Investors and property owners began designing their spaces and optimizing their listings to attract more bookings, which led to the rise of the "Airbnb look." Picture white walls, minimalist decor, mid-century modern furniture, and neutral tones. Quirky, lived-in authenticity was very quickly replaced with this new universally appealing look. It worked...and continues to work.

This is also happening to cities as a whole. As design trends spread, good design is no longer a differentiator that makes one well-designed place stand out. It is now becoming the problem.

As a kid, I remember going into restaurants with my family, and I'd immediately size up the place and start redesigning it in my head. I'd question why the waiting area was laid out the way it was. I'd want to change the font on the menu and declutter the counter. I'd want to change out the lighting, and that artwork by the bathroom had to go. Clearly I was a designer, but I just didn't know it yet. Within minutes, I would subconsciously redesign the entire restaurant. I was a kid with no design experience who knew nothing about the owners, their culture, or their food. I just thought I knew what looked good.

I think we all naturally do the same thing to a degree. We see a struggling downtown, and we know exactly how we'd fix it. Why don't they just hang some string lights across Main Street, add some seating in front of the shops, paint a mural? And yes, in most cases, our knee-jerk instant redesign probably would be an improvement. Good and on-trend design isn't a problem when it comes to small things and campaigns, but when you are approaching your entire brand identity, you can't simply take on the look and messaging of the moment.

I even see this in celebrated place-branding case studies. I may be a little snobby, but these aren't really place brands at all. They are simply place marketing campaigns with good on-trend design. A city's name or development in the font and color palette of the moment may look great. It may even excite and inspire people to go there and create some momentum, but let's not confuse that with a place brand.

There are projects and times where that is exactly what is needed, so I'm not suggesting that quick visual identity refreshes aren't good and don't make sense. My only advice is that before we critique, we pause, and before we design, we listen. Even if it's just for a moment, you need to ask yourself, or better yet, ask the community or audience you are designing for, what makes this place unique? Why are you here? What about its history, culture, or people makes this place special? How can we use design to improve this place in a way that is authentic to the place? Then design.

When we work with communities on a year-long branding project, the entire first six months are spent listening, engaging, and researching before we ever design a single thing. We do a lot more listening than talking. Our team is talented and has a great eye. We could easily fly into a city, walk around for an hour, and immediately start making recommendations and applying good design. In fact, we could probably do that just by zooming around on Google Earth and looking at photos of your town. In some cases, it's really hard to resist that urge to start immediately prescribing and improving. However, we believe, given the importance of a place, we don't just need this place to look a little better. We need the place brand to arm the community to tackle some really big challenges.

Now, this doesn't mean communities should delay progress by spending years on a study, and they definitely don't need to become caricatures of themselves in an effort to be unique. It's very easy to try to be too unique and end up latching on to a gimmick or quality that may be unique but isn't going to capture an entire diverse community. I'm sure you've seen it on HGTV when someone is getting a home makeover. The homeowners are meeting with the designers at the start of the show, and someone casually mentions they like the beach or the Beatles. Cut to the big reveal at the end of the show and their newly designed house is filled with seashells and fishing nets or covered in Beatlemania.

Many cities fall into this trap. In an attempt to be unique and stand out, they fixate on one hyper-specific thing, hoping it will define them. I call this the *roadside attraction approach* to place branding, where a town stakes its identity on having something like the world's largest ball of twine.

Now, our client, High Point, North Carolina, has one of these. It's the largest chest of drawers as they are known as the furniture capital of the world. It's a chest the size of a three-story house with a twenty-foot sock hanging out of one of the drawers. It's funny, and you'll definitely stop by and grab a picture if you're there. But that isn't and can't be their identity. That doesn't mean you can't have these things, as they can be fun, but they absolutely can't be the identity of your community.

The largest frying pan, the largest ball of twine, the pie capital of the world, the biggest Paul Bunyan statue - these are all fine, and I'm not picking on them, as they can capture an element of your history and provide a photo op. But what about that makes someone want to live there? What about it makes someone want to start a business there? You can't center your identity around that. A place needs to offer a lot more than a two-second detour. It needs to be a living, breathing reflection of the people that shape it and offer something they can all see themselves in. Place branding shouldn't be about the biggest, weirdest, or most unusual claim to fame. I do think you can lean into and play with that though. Roswell, New Mexico, does a great job of this with a UFO in their logo and their "We Believe" messaging, but they've made it more than a roadside attraction. They've leaned into it in a way that makes sense for residents and business owners so it can be the cornerstone of their identity. It's a clever brand platform that isn't just saying, "We believe in UFOs." They are building off of that since many people know them for that but channeling that messaging to say, "We Believe in Aerospace," "We Believe in Arts," "We Believe in Ranching." They've made it meaningful for their many different audiences and residents.

Authenticity isn't about leaning into gimmicks and trying to claim one thing that no other place can claim. It's about understanding what makes a place special.

So yes, design is getting better, but good design that's all the same and that's everywhere, I argue, isn't good. I want well-designed places in my town and I want to visit well-designed places in your town, but I want your places to be slightly different from mine.

This doesn't mean everything has to be so on the nose. A coffee shop in Santa Fe doesn't have to become a stereotypical version of the city's identity, overflowing with every imaginable Santa Fe inspired detail. I remember floating down the river with a rafting guide who asked me what I do for a living. I told him that we work with cities on branding and mentioned we were working on a project with Santa Fe. He jokingly said, "I'm thinking turquoise!"

Subtlety in design is good, and not every business needs to mirror a town's identity. You can have a modern coffee shop in a historic town. Businesses don't have to fall in line with the overall aesthetic of their town. There's a difference between a shop creating its own identity and lifting its identity from globalized design trends. The goal isn't for every business to be a replica of the town it's in but rather to contribute, through its own unique identity, to the overall sense of authenticity. By doing that, it naturally becomes authentically Santa Fe, not because it imitates a stereotype of Santa Fe but because it simply exists in Santa Fe and embraces its own genuine character. If you're in Santa Fe and you're authentic, then you are authentically Santa Fe. You are now contributing to what Santa Fe is.

When every place looks the same, we lose something far greater than aesthetics. We lose identity. And identity is worth protecting. A *civic* brand seeks to understand, celebrate, promote, and protect that authentic identity.

## The Ethical Case

The next reason in the case for place branding is the ethical case. The way in which many places have either approached or neglected place branding has led to situations that are harming locals and the environment.

Too often branding, marketing, and development are short sighted and extractive. Place branding is most often used as a way to sell a place and to attract visitors and investment, which, if done in a way that is sustainable and ultimately improves the community for locals, is great. However, too often it is done in a way that is extractive rather than beneficial to the local community.

As a result, we end up pushing out the very residents that built these places, defined its culture, and made it attractive in the first place. We end up overwhelming once authentic destinations with mass tourism, and we exploit local and natural resources. Additionally, because of a shortsighted approach to building our communities, we are strapping local municipalities with financial burdens that feel good in the short term but can be devastating in the long run.

These issues can be the result of an extractive approach to place branding as well as from failing to do place branding at all. Remember, "Fail to plan, plan to fail." You could equally say, "Failing to brand is branding to fail."

A very real example of this is with gentrification. Gentrification is a very complex issue. There are a lot of neighborhoods and places that desperately need to be improved and revitalized, but careful attention needs to be given so that we don't simply push out the very people that have created and shaped that community for generations.

Many would view it as a win if place branding improved the aesthetics, property values, and income of a neighborhood. Those are all good things. The problem with gentrification isn't progress. It's power and ownership. Who benefits from these improvements? It's problematic when anyone gets pushed or priced out, but what I think is even worse is when those that significantly contribute to what makes a place great are pushed out. As they leave, so does the culture and community they built. This often goes back to ownership. If ownership were accessible, they would benefit from the improvements rather than get displaced by them.

A *civic* brand starts with the people that call that place home and focuses on surfacing, prioritizing, and implementing strategies and policies that improve the place while benefitting those locals. Most people don't see how place branding plays a role in things like housing policy and ownership, but that's because they view place branding as just place marketing. When done right, place branding doesn't just raise a place's profile. Instead, it raises the standard of living for the people already there and ensures that revitalization leads to opportunity rather than displacement. We'll dive deeper into exactly how in Chapter 6.

Like gentrification, overtourism is another problem that results from an extractive approach to place branding. Tourism when done right is a win–win that boosts the local economy and gives locals an opportunity to show off their destination in a profitable way. Overtourism is a lot like food shortages. There is enough food in the world to feed everyone, but the problem is access and distribution. There are enough great places in the world to visit. The problem is everyone wants to go to the same spots at the same time. It happens with cities, trails, and restaurants.

When this happens, locals no longer benefit from tourism. Short-term rentals take up all of the housing stock, and it becomes a strain on the local infrastructure and environment. It degrades the quality of life for those that call that place home. Residents soon find that their community is no longer designed for them and is instead designed for visitors.

Overtourism isn't just happening in international destinations like Barcelona, where residents have taken to shooting visitors with water pistols in protest while chanting, "Tourists go home!" It's also happening, ironically, on trails and outdoor destinations, where there should be an abundance of space and opportunities yet everyone is attracted to the same spot due largely to social media. The same channels, voices, and influencers that encouraged people to get out there to discover unique places are now accelerating their overuse because so many people have honed in on the same very specific locations and photo op spots.

Tourism isn't the problem. It's an extractive approach to tourism that treats places as consumable experiences with a focus only on short-term profits rather than long-term sustainability that is the problem.

Many people would blame place branding for overtourism, but once again, that is a result of an extractive approach to place branding that fails to take a triple bottom line approach. Doing it right involves understanding your destination, defining goals, understanding capacities, and being intentional about education, disbursement and distribution, conservation, and policy. Gentrification and overtourism are very complex issues. A destination can't expect to conduct a yearlong place-branding exercise and solve those problems. However, you will never solve those problems without a place brand. It is the foundational step that arms you with the direction and momentum to solve the big challenges.

## The Economic Case

When it comes to the economic case, I'm going to skip, for now, the value of attracting the right kind of investment to your community and the value of attracting visitors that fill your hotels, patronize your local shops, and eat at your local restaurants. I'm going to skip the financial value of attracting and retaining talent and businesses. I'm skipping them not because they aren't important but because everyone already knows these things. They know there is economic benefit to those things, and therefore they are often the only reason that many places do take on place branding. Instead, I want to focus on less considered things that make a very important economic case for place branding.

Too often cities prioritize growth at all costs. As cities seek short-term economic gains, they are simultaneously creating long-term financial and environmental liabilities. They celebrate new subdivisions, shopping centers, and infrastructure without considering if that growth and investment is sustainable in the long run. This kind of growth requires huge investments in roads, utilities, and public services, but the revenue generated in new taxes rarely covers the costs of maintaining it over time. When this happens, cities have to continuously attract development just to be able to afford maintaining what they've already built. This type of growth isn't just financially irresponsible but has environmental consequences as our cities expand and pave over farmland, wetlands, and forest and eliminate the natural systems that feed us, protect us from fires and floods, and filter our water. This type of growth and expansion also leads to longer commutes, which means more emissions.

While this type of non-sustainable development may not be news to those inclined to read a book about place, I think what may be news is the role place branding can and should play in addressing these issues. There are many cities that view this kind of growth as a sign of success, and it could be if you turn a blind eye to the impacts on people, profit, and place and only measure success by the amount of new development and population growth. However, even that is not economic success if you can't afford it in the long haul.

A *civic* brand helps redefine success not by the number of ribbon cuttings but by the health, sustainability, and identity of the place itself. A *civic* brand is first and foremost about alignment, and therefore it helps a community create a shared framework that connects planning, policy, and investment that leads to a clear vision. This arms a community with the power to say no to development and projects that aren't aligned with that vision and say yes to projects that support its values. This quickly shifts the focus away from growth for growth's sake and instead toward the right kind of growth. By first shaping how a city sees itself and then how others see it, a *civic* brand will help guide growth that actually works for the community.

## A *civic* brand leads with clarity and intention.

Another often overlooked aspect is how a place's perception and identity places a ceiling on the economic potential of everything and everyone in the community.

Consider a large employer trying to recruit top talent to come work for their company. They may offer competitive salaries and benefits, but if their city has a negative identity and is perceived as having nothing to do or offering a low quality of life, that employer will likely struggle to recruit the best talent to move there and take the job.

The same applies to your local hospital that is trying to attract world-class doctors and nurses, universities that are looking to recruit students and faculty, and small businesses that are looking to find quality employees and a customer base that can support their business. If a place lacks a strong identity, every organization within that community will be impacted.

On the flip side, a well-branded place can raise that ceiling, making it easier to attract talent and have a solid local market that can patronize your businesses. This is the key reason why place branding isn't just a project for the city government, tourism entity, or economic development organizations to tackle alone. Instead, it should be a collective effort with major employers, hospitals and healthcare systems, school districts and universities, and small businesses all having a seat at the table and involved in the process. These entities all have a stake in the success of the place because they are all limited by its identity, and so they should have a stake in shaping that identity.

When the responsibility of place branding is shared across all of these key players, it's not just easier but it's more impactful because the shared message gets amplified by the many different organizations and entities. It also leads to a more authentic place brand because it's not just led by the government but is shaped by the people and organizations that live, work, and invest in the community.

## The Strategic Case

While there are almost endless reasons in the case for place branding, the last one that I want to touch on here is the strategic case. Place branding offers a decision-making framework that helps leaders make decisions more clearly and confidently, points them in the right direction, and provides efficiency that saves time and money.

Without a clearly defined brand, cities are forced to make hundreds of ad-hoc decisions that can feel disconnected and overwhelming, like playing a game of whack-a-mole. A new initiative gets launched under its own identity that doesn't fit existing efforts, a campaign rolls out that may look good but doesn't align with any overall strategy, a department creates its own website and social channels, and certain projects are approved because they sound good while others aren't because there are no longer funds. Over time these fragmented efforts create confusion instead of clarity. A strong brand can align all of these efforts so they aren't simply in response to political pressure, personal taste, or the loudest voices in the room.

Having a strategic reason backing all of these decisions is incredibly important given the inevitable negative comments that will always come. There will always be critics, especially in this toxic social media era we are living in. However, if leaders have made decisions based on a place-brand vision that is rooted in deep community engagement and strategy, you can be confident in your decisions and won't cave to those comments. The comments will unfortunately still come, but the strategy will give you thicker skin, making you more confident to stand by your decisions and do the right thing.

In addition to more purposeful decision making, a well-defined visual identity, which is just one very small part of a place brand, leads to cost savings through efficiency. Cities waste thousands of dollars on logos, websites, messaging, and staff time for individual departments and initiatives only to end up with a disjointed mess of identities. According to a 2020 *Fast Company* article, the City of Chicago estimates it will save up to $10 million a year by unifying the design of twenty-nine different departments under a single brand. Again, this example speaks to just the visual identity component of a place brand.

This doesn't just eliminate costs that come from this duplication and reinventing of the wheel with each website, slide deck, and graphic that needs to be created, but it also strengthens the brand by creating more consistency. This doesn't mean there isn't a time and a place for different departments and initiatives to take on their own identity. There should be a strategic reason and defined brand architecture that leads to that, not just because one person thought it would be a good idea or simply wanted it. After all, police and fire need to look like police and fire, not just another department. But a place brand strategy makes decisions like these part of a big-picture strategy and not ad-hoc decisions.

The places that have lost their identities, been overrun by tourism, seen locals get priced out of their own neighborhoods, found themselves in a community with a low economic ceiling, and been reactive to ad-hoc decisions weren't victims of branding. They were victims of their community's failure to brand in the first place.

Every place, whether thriving, struggling, or somewhere in between, needs a strategy for telling its story, defining its values, and aligning decisions with its vision. Because if a community doesn't take ownership of its identity, someone else will.

# Chapter 4: Power & Responsibility

Place is important, and I hope I've at least started to make the case for the role place branding can play in shaping our places. But who does that? Who holds the power? Who should lead a place-branding effort?

Cities are the summation of public and private efforts that no single person or entity fully controls. Local and state governments oversee infrastructure, zoning, and public services, creating the foundation that shapes a community, while private businesses, developers, and institutions shape our places through the buildings, businesses, and offerings our communities have. And individual residents and advocacy groups play their own role as they have a level of influence on both governments and businesses in that they choose whom to vote for, where to live, where to spend money, where to work, and what matters to them. Our places are pulled in a million different directions by these different forces, and power is distributed across different players, including elected officials, business leaders, property owners, and engaged citizens, who each play their own role in shaping policies and investments that shape and define the culture and identity of our places.

A city government has a brand, and that city also has a place brand. In some ways, those are the same thing, and in some ways, those are very different things. The municipal organization has its own identity, its own culture, and its own vision. It operates in that way like an individual organization or a business, not a place. It has administration, departments, and staff. On the other hand, a city or county government is actively shaping and influencing the physical environment that it is tasked with managing, and it does so through land use, design and building codes, and streetscapes and by directly shaping what developers can and can't do. It is also shaping the cultural environment through public services, events, arts, recreation, parks, and its policies and budgets. So when you think of the brand of a city, are you thinking about the brand of the city government or the brand of the place? It's probably a blended combination of both. It's a really blurry line as they are the same thing and yet different things. What about a destination marketing organization (DMO) or economic development organization (EDO) that is putting out a place brand but doing so just from their angle? While there is only one place, you can see how there can very quickly be multiple entities all trying to say what that place is.

Someone may love their town but not care for their city government. I have great respect for the public servants that choose to lead and shape our cities. However, we live in an era and a climate, largely driven by national politics, where people have a general distrust or dislike of any form of government. They think, without knowing too much about the details, that the government is incompetent, is wasteful, and has their own agenda, and on both sides of any issue, they often blame the city. "The city" is often referred to in a sort of nebulous way, especially when used to cast blame.

At best, I think people have appreciation for their city government and the work they do, but they view the place they live and call home as something different. They view their place as something separate from the organizational entity that occupies the town hall and is the keeper of that place.

So there absolutely is a difference between a city government brand and a place brand. And there are times when it makes sense to simply focus on a refresh or repositioning of the municipality brand. There are also times when it makes sense to focus on the place brand and not touch the municipality brand and to intentionally keep those very separate. However, a city government brand still needs to capture the vision of the place, and a true place brand still needs critical buy-in and connection with the city government. So they are the same but different. Clear as mud, right?

The city government is definitely the closest thing to a single organization or entity that truly shapes a place brand, but it's hardly the only thing. They can't do anything without private businesses, private developers, universities, school districts, and health care systems. City councils are elected and voted in or out by their residents. When it comes to shaping the perception of a community to external audiences, your DMOs and EDOs are the ones with the budgets that are focusing on external markets. At the end of the day, no single entity is solely in charge, and yet making significant moves on a place brand requires collective action. Responsibility to shape a place also doesn't fall on just one group. It belongs to everyone that interacts with and cares about that place.

• • •

As a result of some of the work our firm was doing, I caught the attention of a prominent Texas businessman, who invited me down to Austin for lunch one day. I won't name his name here, but it's a name that many people would recognize.

The lunch was at a place called the Headliners Club, and I was told to wear a suit. The Headliners Club is an invite-only, membership-based restaurant, sort of like a country club with no golf course. It sits on the twenty-first floor of a building in downtown Austin, Texas. The Headliners Club was founded in 1954 by Charles E. Green, who was a longtime executive editor of the *Austin American-Statesman*, and on their own website, they describe the Headliners Club as "a comfortable environment for those who make the headlines and those who write the headlines."

I drove down to Austin, parked in the valet, and rode up the elevator to the twenty-first floor. As the mirrored doors of the elevator closed, I saw the reflection of myself in my cheap, ill-fitting suit that I only wear every few years for a funeral. I'm not a suit guy, and it was pretty obvious. The elevator opened, and my host was standing there waiting for me. As we walked to our table, he gave me a mini tour and history lesson of the club. The dining room had wood-clad walls and fully set formal dining tables with more glasses and silverware than I ever know what to do with and which they always seem to take away as soon as I order. There was a prestigious library of books and famous artwork, including two notorious nude paintings, one of Marilyn Monroe and one of Jayne Mansfield, in the men's restroom. Story has it that the Marilyn Monroe painting has been stolen multiple times over the years but somehow always magically returns. The dining room was full of journalists, state senators, U.S. senators, and, I've heard, the occasional celebrity. In a room like this, I imagine the celebrities that show up are very likely the most known yet least powerful people in the room. It's the who's who of the powerful and elite, very much like the famous Texas businessman who invited me there.

What really struck me as I walked through the room learning about the club, having influential people pointed out to me, and overhearing fragments of conversations and business negotiations was the realization that these discussions were shaping the future in profound ways. Decisions were being made in real time, and these are the people calling the shots, impacting policy, impacting development at large scale, and who have historically been shaping our places.

After we ate, as I was waiting for my host to finish up in the restroom, I walked over to the window, leaned against the glass, and looked down at the streets of Austin below. As I looked down, I saw people going about their daily routines. There was a drummer loading his drums out of a van and into a club, a business owner arranging chairs outside their shop, and people waiting on crossing signals to cross the street on their way back to work from lunch.

My first thought was, *What am I doing up here?* And my second thought was a realization that all the people down below were going about their day like busy ants working hard to do what they thought they needed to do to shape their lives, their businesses, and their community. However, what was truly shaping their world wasn't happening down on the street and instead was happening up here, in the Headliners Club. Significant decisions about the city and its economy, development, and policies were being discussed behind these closed doors up on the twenty-first floor by powerful politicians and business leaders. While the people below were focused on their own small contributions, the power felt like it was all up here.

Were the busy ants truly shaping their community or were they more like puppets down on the ground? Did I just have lunch with the puppet masters? I left a little unsettled with the belief that those in the Headliners Club were the ones who actually owned everything and the people down below were the ones that would end up eternally paying. In many ways, that is how most places work. While that's kind of a depressing reality, I have seen signs of the scales slowly tipping or at least evening out in a constant push and pull of power.

You can't fabricate art. You can't fabricate culture. And a lot of developers and politicians that are trying to maximize profits have realized that these massive, multi-million dollar mixed use real estate developments need art and culture to be profitable. They need a sense of place and they need culture, so they attempt to fabricate it.

I'm sure you've seen it in your community. New developments mimic the architecture of varying facade heights to make what is really a single building all owned by one developer look like an organic Main Street built over time with different buildings and multiple owners. Now that murals aren't just viewed as graffiti and instead something that contributes to the culture of a place, we are seeing all these corporate, faux murals popping up on the side of a Whole Foods or brand new apartment complex.

They're recognizing that the things those ants or puppets down on the street were doing all contribute to the quality and culture of place, and they are desperately trying to appeal to that and replicate it because for all the power up in that club, those are things they haven't fully figured out how to purchase or fabricate.

I think that's a good thing. Not the faux facades, soulless developments, and fake murals, but the fact that the power is shifting, if even just a little bit. The fact that there is recognition of the value of art and culture shifts the power ever so slightly back down to the people on the streets rather than being held solely by those up in the Headliners Club. They are learning financial lessons that those things are important and can't be faked.

The fact the developers, CEOs, and politicians are learning that lesson was confirmed by a story that was told to me by another storied Texan, this one by Rick Perry, the former Governor of Texas. He told me the story of a Fortune 500 company that was looking to relocate their headquarters to Dallas, Texas, back in the eighties, which was a couple decades before his time as governor. This corporate headquarters relocation would have been a significant economic development win for the City of Dallas and for the State of Texas.

While he never told me the name of the company, I was told it was a large company. It would have meant a lot of jobs, a lot of home buyers, and a boon to the economy from the ripple effect of such a big corporate move. It would have been in the news and celebrated by politicians, economic development, and chambers of commerce all taking credit for making it happen and "creating jobs." It would have been viewed as a major win.

The deal was at the finish line, and the CEO and his wife flew into Dallas for what was supposed to be one final visit before the deal was signed and made official. Apparently everyone involved viewed it as more of a victory lap than a final decision-making trip.

The story has it that the CEO's wife visited Dallas on that final trip and during the trip said to her husband, "There's no culture here. There's no art." And with that, the deal was lost.

Now, this was decades ago, and at the time, downtown Dallas was dominated by a pretty sterile business culture during the day, and it was dead at night and on weekends. She was right. There was no art, and there was no culture.

Since then, Dallas has radically changed things, investing in what is now the largest contiguous urban arts district in the nation, spanning 118 acres. The Dallas Arts District is home to an impressive collection of cultural and community assets, including the Booker T. Washington High School for the Performing and Visual Arts, Crow Museum of Asian Art, Dallas Black Dance Theatre, Dallas Museum of Art, Dallas Symphony Orchestra, Dallas Theater Center, Moody Performance Hall, Meyerson Symphony Center, Nasher Sculpture

Center, and Klyde Warren Park, and is a vibrant hub for art, performance, and urban life. People now actually live downtown and go downtown.

That was a lesson that Texas and Dallas learned the hard way, but I think it's an inspiring story because it shows again the power of culture, even if the power hasn't completely shifted. Many of those things that Dallas invested in were big things, not small things, but they are important, and you can't replicate them with money alone. You can build the theaters, performance halls, and art schools with power and money, but it takes artists and everyday people to fill those spaces and make them successful. You can't fabricate art and culture. You need to get the artists, the residents, and the average person involved. They need to love their place and start collectively shaping their place.

I'm not saying you don't need money and that you don't need investors, developers, and politicians as those things are very important, but when you get the balance right, that's when a place can really thrive. Developers, politicians, and money can be the gasoline on the fire, but you have to have that authentic spark that comes from the people.

• • •

Traditionally, economic development was all about recruiting companies. If you could get the company, then you got the jobs, and that's how you got the people and the economic activity that came with it. While that approach is very much still in play and cities still fork over millions in tax breaks and incentives to recruit companies, things have changed a bit.

A famous example of this is the whole Amazon HQ2 debacle, which led to competition between cities for the promised billions in investment and thousands of jobs. Hundreds of cities across the country created proposals and campaigns, where they offered tax breaks, incentives, and even renaming parts of their cities. When Amazon announced its selection, which was actually two cities, New York City (Long Island City) and Arlington, Virginia, it was no surprise that both were already significant talent hubs with vast pools of educated workers. The backlash over subsidies led Amazon to abandon its New York plans and focus just on Arlington, and even that became a partial move. This made it pretty clear that Amazon already knew where it was going, and most cities competing never stood a chance. Instead, Amazon was just fishing for the biggest incentives from places they already wanted to go. It all came down to where the people were.

Economic development has shifted, where it's at least a little less about attracting the big company first and is more about attracting the talent. The way you attract talent is through quality of life, placemaking, and the little things that matter to people in their daily lives. People still need jobs, but places have learned that if we create places that people want to be, companies, jobs, and economic activity will follow.

So who's really in control? Is it the politicians and developers pulling the strings from behind closed doors or is it the everyday people down on the street?

In *The Responsible Company*, Yvon Chouinard argues that historically there have been three forces that have shaped society: the federal government, local government, and civil democracy. Then, in the late nineteenth century, corporations entered the mix and added a fourth force. Despite the money and politics that come with three of those four, Chouinard makes the case that civil democracy is still the strongest because even when governments or corporations take action, it is usually in response to pressure from the people. He gives several examples throughout history that prove the point.

The expansion of national parks, Yosemite National Park, and the protection of wilderness wasn't simply a top-down decision by Teddy Roosevelt. Instead, it was driven by conservationist John Muir, who convinced Roosevelt of its value by taking him to visit and camp under the giant sequoias. The Civil Rights Movement wasn't driven by political leaders that simply thought we needed change. It was due to everyday people that refused to accept segregation and injustice, which then forced the government to respond.

So who holds the power of place today? Is it still the politicians and multi-million dollar developers or is it the resident, the artist, the makers, the average person? I think it's both, but the scales are leveling out as we better recognize the role of each. The most transformative changes rarely start in city hall. Real change starts on the ground with people that care and have civic pride for the community and demand something better.

So while the conversations in the Headliners Club were shaping the city's policies and economic direction, the real identity of the place - the art, music, businesses, and culture - was happening down on the streets below. And while those people weren't at the table where the major decisions were being made, their influence couldn't be ignored. If those in power wanted to create places people actually cared about and wanted to live in, then they would be forced to understand and respect the energy, creativity, and authenticity happening at street level. This push and pull between those that build the structures of a place and those that inhabit it and give it life is at the heart of every city's evolution.

# A *civic* brand doesn't imitate culture, it reflects and serves it.

Let's build places for people, and the politicians and developers will follow as they'll want to invest where the people are and create places that are attractive and beautiful for everyone. They're still very much in the mix and very much shaping things, but it's more of a balance.

• • •

If we recognize the ever-shifting push and pull of power in shaping our places and that multiple entities and organizations all play a key role in shaping the identity, then who has the responsibility to bring all these different players together and cast that shared vision for a community? Is it the city government? The DMO or EDO?

While there isn't a single right or wrong answer, the places that are getting it right aren't just putting the ownership squarely on one organization or one entity. They're collaborative or in some cases through a more formal co-op that involves all those different entities and players all coming together to push a place forward, creating something that not any one of them fully owns but that they can all buy into and everyone benefits from.

In a talk that I regularly give, I often play a short video clip of fifty people all trying to surf the same wave. It's a silly video, and it's chaotic as they're crashing into each other, falling down, and in each other's way. They're all trying to do the same thing. They're trying to ride the wave, but it's a mess. This is how our cities can feel as city governments, DMOs, economic development organizations, chambers of commerce, realtors, individual businesses, hospitals, and school districts are all out there trying to promote the same place but doing it on their own and in fifty different ways.

This also happens even within a single organization, especially within city and county governments with multiple departments. While it is one city or one county, numerous departments are often doing their own thing. They are creating their own department brands, style guides, websites, taglines, and social media accounts, so they, too, are like the surfers in the video, all trying to do their own thing but crashing into each other. As mentioned before, there is absolutely a time and place for more complex brand architecture that allows sub-brands, but this lack of alignment and strategy not only wastes resources but also dilutes the message, making it harder to actually communicate or create any real sense of identity.

A place brand has to be bigger than the term limits of any one city council member or civic leader. It needs to come from the collective will of the community to ensure it has the staying power to survive the inevitable changes in leadership. While local governments can certainly take the lead in initiating and organizing a place-branding process, it's essential for other major organizations, civic entities, and the broader public to be involved. True buy-in happens when these groups are not just engaged in the process but also have a financial stake in its success. At a minimum, they must be involved in shaping the vision and take an active role in championing the process and implementation. Collaborative workshops that get these entities in the room together are one of the very best ways to start this process and for them to all begin to recognize their shared and vested interests in making it happen while understanding that it's much more than a campaign or short-term project.

# A *civic* brand is not a campaign,
# it's a commitment.

While a comprehensive plan can be a natural opportunity to establish or revisit a city's vision, planning firms that develop comp plans are primarily focused on future land use and development guidance, and therefore the vision portion of those plans is ironically not that comprehensive. A true vision that drives a place brand extends far beyond the level of vision statement that you typically find in a comprehensive plan, which most could easily apply to any city as they simply speak to quality of life and safety in fairly generic terms. For this reason, we believe that in a perfect scenario, branding efforts should lead, and all subsequent planning efforts, such as comprehensive plans, downtown master plans, and so on, should follow. That said, if your community just completed a comp plan update, that doesn't mean you can't start the place-branding process. Regardless of timing, simply starting the process is what is important. If yesterday was the best time, today is the second best.

The city government definitely can be the tip of the spear and lead a place-branding project, and there are great examples of that, but we can't expect city governments to go it alone. We ask way too much of our city governments already, and we give them way too little to actually do what we demand. We expect municipalities to provide essential services, like fire and police, and maintain roads and utilities. We also expect them to create and manage parks, recreation programs, and events while simultaneously fostering economic development, planning for future growth, and addressing issues like housing. Despite all of these demands, nobody likes paying taxes, and therefore cities are often underfunded.

Cities have the upward pressure from demanding residents and businesses and the downward pressure from state and national mandates that often require more work and expenses yet don't come with the necessary funding to pull it all off. We need to get universities, large employers, small business owners, realtors, chambers of commerce, DMOs, developers, and all of the key players whose success is ultimately capped by the success of the place to come together. They need to work together and not operate in silos. They're all together, pushing a place forward. So yes, a city can lead a place-branding effort, but it absolutely can't do it alone.

Now that we've explored why place matters and how it shapes our lives, the next questions to answer are, how do we shape our places in return, and how do we use place branding to solve those big challenges our places are facing?

In Part II, we'll get clear on what a place brand is and what it isn't and arm you with the approach that will help you not create just another place brand designed to market a destination but instead create a *civic* brand, one that serves as a framework for decision making, aligns and inspires stakeholders, and makes your place the best version of itself.

# PART II: ANATOMY OF A BRAND

## Chapter 5: The Foundation

If you've spent much time around designers, branding consultants, or marketers, you've likely heard this phrase a hundred times: "A brand isn't a logo." It's become a bit of a game to me now, like an internal bingo that only I'm playing. There are several phrases on my personal bingo board: "A brand isn't a logo," "we don't make plans that sit on a shelf," and "we don't make cookie cutter plans." These are phrases that people confidently say hundreds of times, all with good intention but with partial accuracy and, most of the time, with very little behind it.

What humors me most about "a brand isn't a logo" isn't that I disagree with it but rather the sequence of events that happens every time it's mentioned. One person says it and everyone laughs in a condescending way, as if to scoff at anyone that thinks a brand is indeed just a logo. By making the statement and then laughing in agreement, everyone is sending a performative signal that they get it, they know what branding really is, and most people don't.

However, as soon as they are done laughing, they often look down at their feet, and then the conversation shifts. It's like they feel the need to show the others they get it, and yet they don't know how to communicate what it really is. They just know what it's not.

I've even seen this play out at branding conferences, where someone between sessions makes that comment/joke and then an hour later is on stage presenting the branding case study of the project that they worked on for a year and a half that comes down to...a logo and tagline.

I'm not trying to pick on anyone. I never say anything. I just play my mental bingo and say to myself, "Yep, there it is," then smile and laugh. After all, it is true. But I genuinely believe that while many people know what a brand isn't, they don't go far enough to understand what it truly is and even more so with place branding.

When people are making the comment that a brand is not just a logo, they are simply making the point that it's not just the visual identity. And they are right in that a brand is not just the logo, colors, and fonts, even though it is commonplace to hear, "We rebranded," or "Check out our new brand," in reference to nothing more than a logo update. Logo updates and a refresh of a visual identity can often be needed, very important, and part of a larger brand strategy. So I definitely don't think we need to get righteous when someone says "brand" when they really just meant logo or visual identity. I do, however, think that it is very important when approaching city branding, district branding, and place branding that we get really clear on if this is a true place-branding project or just an update of the visual identity.

You may not be revisiting the vision, values, story, strategy, experience, and entire essence of what your place is all about. You may simply be looking to update the visual identity. There is nothing wrong with that, and in a lot of cases, that makes a lot of sense. Perhaps it's simply outdated or over time there has become too many variations of your visual identity, with different details, colors, or fonts that you simply need to reset and lock in a new official version. Perhaps you need to rein in some sub-brands or need to refine your visual identity so it works better across different platforms, whether that means creating a responsive logo system for different sizes and channels or simply refreshing your templates and style guide.

If it is more than that, and if you are looking to get at the essence and understanding of who you are as a place, what your story is, where you are headed, and how that should shape your environment, policies, and messaging - well, now you are looking at addressing much more than just the visual identity. You're now talking about a true place brand.

It's common to hear that a place brand is essentially the overall perception of a place. While perception isn't actually synonymous with a place brand, it is a key component. The perception of a place exists whether you've lived there forever, if you've been there for one minute, and even if you've never been there. A place still has a perception of it, even if it's a place you've never heard of.

What is your perception of Nauru? Even if you've never heard of it, you'll still form some instant perception based on the name and the fact that you haven't heard of it. What are you picturing? A bustling city in an African country? A remote Pacific island? Whatever comes to mind, it's shaped by the way names trigger associations even when we know nothing about a place. If you google it, you'll have a new perception shaped by the Google search results, which will show photos, their flag, a map, and the weather.

Nauru is the third smallest country in the world and is a tiny island in the Pacific. It has white sand beaches that are lined with palm trees and, interestingly, has no capital city. Is that what you pictured?

What is your perception of New Orleans? With a place you know, and especially if you've been there, your perception will be shaped by hundreds, likely thousands, of additional factors, and your brain, like the super computer that it is, will calculate and weigh all those individual factors in an instant algorithm to arrive at your perception. You could start to try to explain it, but it would be impossible to fully communicate everything that shaped your perception.

Some have tried to put a value on place branding. What they have really done is put a value on perception. The flaw in that approach is that there is perception whether you actively do any place branding or not. Whether you attempt to shape it or not, it's there. Geography, weather, history, local economy, built environment, experiences - those things all exist with or without place branding.

Therefore, you can't simply say the value of place branding is equal to the value of perception on a local economy. Instead, the value of place branding is in between that current perception and how much you can influence that perception. Can you improve or strengthen the perception? Can you shift perception in a way that benefits the community? And better yet, instead of simply taking a place as is and working to improve the perception, can you actually improve the place itself, which in turn improves the perception in a more authentic way?

That's the power of place branding. There is absolutely value in that. It's not just about shaping perception alone, but it's about strategically and very intentionally shaping the place.

Perception is built on thousands of factors, and it's different for everyone. The weather, the politics, the taxes, the food, the architecture - different people value different things, which means the way they perceive a place will never be exactly the same. Additionally, everyone has personal experiences that shape that perception as well. You may have drank too much and got sick on Bourbon Street, and that shapes your perception. You may have had your favorite meal ever there, and that shapes your perception.

The assumption that a place brand is just perception is why many people get branding and marketing confused, because shaping the perception also sounds a lot like marketing. So even if they know a brand isn't just the logo, they may move on to all the marketing efforts that are attempting to shape the perception, like messaging and storytelling, and assume that is the rest of what branding is.

The visual identity is part of it but not all of it. Marketing and storytelling are also part of it but definitely not all of it. So what's left? The place itself.

The Apple brand isn't just a logo. The Apple brand also isn't just the advertisements and commercials for their projects. Their visual identity and marketing certainly play a role in shaping your perception, but the heavy lifting is done by the product itself and your experiences with it such as how it feels to walk into an Apple store, how it feels to open that new iPhone box, the user experience of the device, the customer support, your take on the company's approach to privacy, your take on where they build their products, how much it costs, and on and on. Every single thing about your experience with Apple shapes their brand, and therefore every decision Apple makes should be driven by their ultimate vision for their brand. For our purposes, the place is the product.

While there are thousands of factors at play, I have developed the following formula to captures what contributes to a place brand. Everything can be categorized under three main categories of Place, Identity, and Marketing. Under each of those main categories, there are multiple subcategories:

### Place Brand = Place x Identity x Marketing

## PLACE

**Built Environment**
Districts & Land Use
Wayfinding
Parks & Trails
Public Spaces
Mobility/Connectivity
Architecture
Housing
Sound

**Culture**
Values
City Services
Politics & Taxes
Economy
Education
Food
People
History

**Assets/Attractions**
Public Art
Events
Hotels & Meeting Spaces
Sports & Entertainment
Universities & Schools
Mass Transit & Airports
Organizations & Non-Profits
Businesses & Retail

**Natural Environment**
Open Spaces
Geography
Weather

# IDENTITY

### Vision
Purpose
Goals

### Brand Strategy
Brand Platform
Brand Story
Positioning
Brand Principles

### Visual Identity
Logos
Colors
Typography
Visual Language
Brand Architecture

### Verbal Identity
Messaging
Tone of Voice
Naming/Vocabulary

# MARKETING

### Content Marketing
Social Media Marketing
Website/Digital Channels
Search Marketing (SEO/SEM)
Email Marketing/Automation
Blogging/Articles
Video Production
Podcasting

### Paid Media
Influencer Marketing
Broadcast Advertising
Digital Advertising
Outdoor Advertising
Print Advertising
Guides/Direct Mail

### Event Marketing
Trade Shows
Conferences
Seminars
Sponsorships
Community Events

### Public Relations
Media Relations
Press Releases
Crisis Management
Internal Communications
External Communications

While there are certainly things that aren't listed here, most of them can find their way under one of these categories or subcategories. This framework of Place Branding = Place × Identity × Marketing is a simplified and structured way to grasp the components that make up a place brand, making it easier to evaluate and refine over time.

To understand place branding, it's important to understand what you control, what you influence, and what you don't control. Within these subcategories under Place x Identity x Marketing, some elements are fully within our control, some we can influence, and others are beyond our control entirely. All of them play a role in shaping perception, even the ones we don't control.

The most obvious factors we don't control are things like geography, history, and weather. Both the perception and brand of mountain towns or beach towns are highly influenced by their geography and weather, which are what they are no matter how much branding work you do.

On the other end of the spectrum are the things you fully control, like the visual identity and marketing tactics. Logos, messaging, social media, websites, and ad campaigns all fall into this category. These are the obvious and most visible and what most people focus on when they think about "branding" a place. While these elements are important, they should be grounded in something deeper.

A good-looking logo or campaign isn't enough on its own as it needs to reflect and reinforce the authentic identity of the place, and that authentic identity is largely shaped by things that fall in the middle category that a place doesn't fully control but can influence. This includes elements like culture, politics, architecture, taxes, public spaces, events, parks, trails, land use, zoning, and housing policy. These factors shape how people experience and interact with a place, and while they aren't typically considered branding elements, a strong place brand should impact all of them. When branding is done well, it doesn't just live in the marketing materials. It also shapes the product and shapes the policies and choices leaders and stakeholders make. A place brand isn't just about how a city or town looks on the surface. It's about the lived experiences and decisions that shape its future and the values it represents.

With place branding, sometimes you're changing or improving the product (your place), and sometimes you're just shaping the messaging or story. Both are important, but the ability to truly shape the product is vital. If you're tasked with place branding, you really have to have a seat at the table to impact the product and not just the messaging around it. Otherwise you're just selling the place.

While this framework of Place x Identity x Marketing provides a foundation for looking at what contributes to a place brand, it does not address whether a place brand is being approached in a way that is sustainable and profitable or if it is equitable and benefits the local community and environment. This is why I advocate for going a step further and applying a triple bottom line approach that considers people, profit, and place as a lens to evaluate and shape our communities.

Traditionally the success of place branding has been measured only through an economic lens that measures the number of visitors, hotel stays, ad impressions, tax revenues, and the economic impact of its efforts. While these metrics are important, they do not tell the whole story. By integrating the triple bottom line approach into place-branding efforts, we can make sure we aren't just promoting our places but are actively making our places stronger, more resilient, and more lovable, and this is what I think makes a place brand become a *civic* brand.

$$A \; Civic \; \text{Brand} = \left( \frac{\text{Place x Identity x Marketing}}{\text{Triple Bottom Line}} \right)$$

The term "triple bottom line" was coined by John Elkington in 1994. John was a sustainability consultant and author and challenged businesses and organizations to consider their impact on society and the environment.

When you take a triple bottom line approach to valuing a company, yes, profit is essential but so is its impact on its people and the planet. If a company is profitable but it's harming the environment and taking advantage of its workers, I would say that it is not a successful company. The same goes for a city or destination. If it's attracting visitors but locals are priced out of their own communities, that's not good for the people. If the amount of tourism and type of development destroys the local fabric and environment, that's certainly not good for the place, regardless of how profitable it is.

Patagonia, the outdoor clothing brand, not the region in South America, is one of the best examples of a company that truly embraces a triple bottom line approach. As a successful and profitable company with decades of consistent performance, Patagonia has demonstrated its ability to navigate shifting fashion and outdoor trends and no doubt checks the "profit" box.

However, in a triple bottom line approach, profitability is not enough. When it comes to the people category, Patagonia does pretty well there too. Patagonia consistently ranks among the best companies to work for and has been a model that other companies have followed when it comes to valuing employee well-being and culture.

The third category is the planet. Patagonia's commitment to the planet is unparalleled in the business world, especially with their fairly recent redefining of their core mission that they are in business to save the planet. They are leaders in sustainable manufacturing and supply chain practices, and they donate considerable profits to environmental causes.

The interesting thing is how these things all work together. Until we start doing business on other planets, a company can't be profitable without our planet and people. We can't provide stable jobs for our people without being profitable and without a healthy planet. Just like Patagonia, I believe that we can't save our planet if we aren't profitable and don't have the resources to tackle big challenges and if our people aren't fully invested and committed. This triple bottom line approach has made Patagonia a leader not just in the outdoor apparel industry but in demonstrating how business can be a force for good.

Just like we shouldn't look at profit alone to define the success of a company, we shouldn't only look at how many visitors a destination brand attracts, how many companies an economic development brand recruits, or how much sales tax a city brand generates. We do value those things, and those are very important for destinations and cities, just as it is vital for a company to be profitable. A company can't benefit its people and the planet if it is bankrupt.

Those that know me know that I'm not a fan of Amazon. Amazon is an extremely profitable company, so just like Patagonia, they check that box. However, in a triple bottom line approach, I think many would agree they fail when it comes to their people and planet. Amazon has faced significant criticism over the years when it comes to how they treat their employees. There are consistently articles and reports coming out about Amazon's poor working conditions and regular strikes and protests by warehouse workers and delivery drivers advocating for safety issues and a better work environment.

While the company has made environmental pledges, such as

committing to net-zero carbon emissions by 2040, its entire business model of fast shipping, massive data centers for AWS, and lots of wasteful packaging leads to a significant carbon footprint. And if we're talking about the impact on place and not just the planet, I view Amazon as a considerable threat to local economies and local businesses. Regardless of your personal stance on Amazon, in a triple bottom line analysis, they definitely are not as successful as when they are measured by profit alone.

While this approach is good for even private companies to take, I think it is imperative for place brands. A *civic* brand values its culture and works to make sure that branding efforts don't just cater to visitors or outside investors. Instead, it views visitors and investors as a way to benefit the locals. It supports a wide range of interests, is economically sustainable, understands that it has to protect its resource base, including the local economy and environment, and is continually striving to be the best version of itself.

# A *civic* brand balances people, profit, and place.

Traditionally branding is very much about control, especially in corporate and product branding, where consistency and carefully controlling the message are fundamental to shaping a brand. This is why brand standards and style guides exist. They create detailed rules for how brand assets should and should not be used. They manage logo usage, typography rules, color palettes, and messaging, all with the goal of consistently presenting an image in order to fully control perception. I have a copy of the 1975 *NASA Graphics*

*Standards Manual* that was turned into a coffee table book, and the level of detail in it is incredible. It's 220 pages of detailed rules on how to apply NASA's visual identity. Branding has long been about defining and enforcing standards.

Place branding is a little different though. We still need to have style guidelines that help present the visual identity in a very consistent way, but when a place brand is meant to represent an entire community and not just the city government or singular entity, there is going to be a lot that you do not control. City governments need to tightly control their brand simply from a communication standpoint so that people know if a message is coming from the official government entity or not. However, a true place brand is owned by the people and not by any one organization. That means it has to be more organic and open to taking on a life of its own.

That doesn't mean a city government can't spearhead a place-brand initiative or develop place-brand strategies that seamlessly tie into the municipality's brand strategy. In fact, that approach of tackling a tightly controlled city government brand within a larger place-brand strategy is one of our favorite projects to tackle.

The reality of elements of a place-brand strategy being out of their control can be unsettling for designers, strategists, and leaders that are used to carefully controlling every detail. Understanding this nuanced control and the balance of public and private is one reason why design agencies that don't specialize in place branding, while they may do brilliant work, aren't qualified or struggle to do place-branding work. It is extremely different from branding companies. We spend years developing strategies, poring over every detail, testing messaging, refining visuals, and creating detailed implementation plans. We get invested and have a very specific vision for how it will go, and then we hand it off to not just to the client but to a community.

Once it's handed over, things get real, and they start to shift and take on a life of their own. The brand gets implemented, adapted, and adjusted in ways you could never anticipate. Sometimes those changes make us cringe because they weren't done how we would have done them, and sometimes we're pleasantly surprised. That is the nature of place branding.

It's a lot like raising kids in that you want to teach, nurture, and protect them, but then, at some point, they grow up and go out into the world to make their own choices. Sure, they'll make mistakes and do things differently than you would have wanted them to, but those mistakes are theirs to own. When they succeed, that success is even greater because it's truly theirs, and that's when they surprise you and do great things you could have never dreamed of. After all, the place eventually has to take ownership of the place brand.

A place brand, at its most successful, is one that no single entity fully controls and takes on that life of its own. City governments are already used to operating in this way because they don't own all the buildings or businesses within a town. They can't dictate every aspect of how a place feels. Cities can only control what they can control, and they use that to influence the development and direction of the community.

## A *civic* brand is shaped by everyone and owned by no one.

One of the best examples of an organic place brand that nobody owns is "Pura Vida" in Costa Rica. If you've been there, then you know exactly what I'm talking about. "Pura Vida" isn't just a tagline or campaign. It's more of a way of life. You'll find "Pura Vida" on everything there. It's on every souvenir, stickers, shop windows, license plate frames, and business signage. People use it as a greeting, and it's what you say when getting your photo taken. If you post photos from a visit to Costa Rica to social media, you'll very likely get comments from friends that have been there before commenting, "Pura Vida!" on your post. What makes it really work is that it's not just a visitor and tourist thing. Yes, it's on all the merch and apparel a visitor would buy, but that's because it's also deeply ingrained in the local Costa Rican culture. It wasn't created by an agency, it's not owned by anyone, and there is no style guide or official logo for it.

When people embrace a brand by making it their own and carry it forward in ways you never could have imagined, that's what makes a place brand great. It needs to be so ingrained that it's bigger than any one mayor, election cycle, city council, or audience. As place leaders, we need to get comfortable operating in a space where we don't control everything and need to focus on creating something people can connect with and that they feel they own and want to carry forward themselves. When a place brand stops being just a marketing effort and becomes an authentic lived identity, this is the true sign of success.

# Chapter 6: People, Profit, Place

Place branding isn't just about shaping perception. It's about shaping reality. Applying a triple bottom line approach to place branding isn't as simple as just saying, "We care about people, profit, and our place." That's much easier to say than it is to do. If a destination marketing organization is tasked with attracting visitors and they develop a place brand that does exactly that, is that a success? Not if it's at the cost of its local people, its environment, its sustainability, and its culture.

There are countless ways in which what can appear to be successful branding has a negative impact on its community. We're certainly not anti-tourism or anti-economic development. In fact, I love working with DMOs on tourism projects, and I love working on economic development projects that attract talent and investment. But when we get hired for a tourism project, it's because the client wants to do those projects in a way that doesn't simply attract more visitors but is authentic, benefits the locals, and respects the history, culture, and environment. When hired for an economic development project, it's not just about outside investment and talent but how that can benefit the locals that are already there. We focus on how we can provide them with tools to be more successful, how it can help employees, and how it can level up the workforce by offering access to capital, training, and tools to build an ecosystem that drives the local economy.

I am the biggest homer for locals and local businesses, so even when we are hired to do a tourism campaign and even if the client is focused only on getting more visitors to fill up hotels, our process starts with understanding how this can benefit the locals. When you visit a place, you're not just going to see their buildings and their attractions. You're going to somebody's home, you're going to somebody's place, and you're going to experience it.

# A *civic* brand guides growth to serve locals.

One of the biggest metrics of success in place branding is whether or not it contributes to a sense of civic pride. First, with the locals, does it make them proud of where they live? And for the visitors, do they gain a sense of pride from the place? Do they want to share and tell others about it? And better yet, do they want to take something home with them? Not just a souvenir but a value, a lesson, or an experience they can take back home to their community to make their place better. That is the essence of a *civic* brand and comes from getting the triple bottom line right.

## *People*

On every project that we've done in cities across the country, there's one thing that always comes up when we ask, "What makes this place special? What makes this place unique?" We get the same answer, whether we're in a big city or a small town and no matter what state we're in. It's always the top answer.

More recently, in a keynote talk that I give, I've started asking audience members what they think it is. Every single time they've guessed right. It's the people. The first several dozen times that we heard "the people," we kind of dismissed it. We thought, *Yeah, I'm sure the people are great, but everyone says that, and if every place says it's the people, then it can't really be the people.* If what makes a place special is the same everywhere, can it really be that special?

It actually took me several years of doing engagement and place branding, talking to thousands of people about what makes their places special and what makes them unique, and crafting stories and narratives that attempt to capture that to truly understand what people meant when they said that. What we learned was that they were right. It often is the people.

But you can't stop there. You have to go much deeper to really understand what specifically about the people is special. That's something that people don't typically have the answer to. They're not able to quickly say it's the people and, when you press further, explain why. They will certainly talk about the sense of community and give anecdotal examples of what it is about the people, but it takes nuanced listening and observation over time to really piece it together. It's one of those things where people know but can't quite put their fingers on it or articulate it. But when you uncover it, package it perfectly, and show it back to a community, they go, "Yes, that's it. You nailed it! That's what we've been trying to say!"

## A *civic* brand is uncovered, not invented.

That is exactly what place branding is all about. It's about engaging, listening to, and understanding people to discover the things that they think, maybe just subconsciously, and are trying to communicate but can't even find the words for and then crafting and giving them the words back. As mentioned in the introduction, this is why we almost never say "rebranding." We believe a brand is already there, and we are simply uncovering it or helping communities rediscover it.

• • •

I live in Salida, Colorado, and the Arkansas River runs right through our small mountain town. The Arkansas River between Buena Vista and Salida runs through Browns Canyon National Monument and is the most commercially rafted section of river in the United States. It also has the longest stretch of Gold Medal waters in Colorado, which is a designation in fly fishing for the amount of quality fish in a given stretch of water. We also have Monarch Mountain, one of the country's last remaining independent ski resorts that doesn't make artificial snow. Salida is also in what is called the Banana Belt because it's warmer than surrounding areas even though our county has more fourteeners, which are mountain peaks that top out at over 14,000 feet, than anywhere else. This makes it so that in the winter, you can ski on the mountain and yet go mountain biking and fly fishing in the valley on the same day.

So in Salida, Colorado, when I look at what makes this place special and therefore what is special about the people in Salida, it is this idea of "guide culture." With all of those river and mountain amenities, it takes a lot of guides. Rafting guides, fly fishing guides, mountain biking guides, ski instructors and ski patrol, horseback riding guides, hunting guides, and naturalists - there are guides for any and every activity you can imagine.

Guides are often helping someone to do something they've never done before. They're having to teach them. They're having to keep them safe. They might be doing something that is hard and scary for someone that has never done it. They're having to make them feel safe and at the same time have fun. They're having to make small talk and make sure that people have an enjoyable time. They're having to work with people from all different backgrounds, cultures, and varying skill sets. However, this guide culture that is prevalent here is not just found surrounding those outdoor activities that people are doing when they come to visit Salida, Colorado, on vacation. Teachers at the high school and middle school, police officers, firefighters, those working in economic development, city government workers, and those running local businesses and restaurants - many of them have some connection back to guiding. For many, it's what originally brought them to Salida. They guided when they were younger and may have moved on to other careers and stages of life, but that guide culture remains. It's why they're here.

When you have a community that's not just full of active guides but full of people that used to be guides that are now doing all different things, it creates a culture, and that culture doesn't just produce things directly related to guiding. It impacts how people talk, their style, their vibe, the art, the music, the food, and the culture. It influences all of those things. It makes Salida, Salida.

So what do you do with that? Does that mean that you just promote guides and guide-related activities in your tourism ads? No. What you need to do with that is define it and protect it. Just like you define and protect architecture that is essential to your history and culture, you need to define and protect what is essential to the culture of your people. It needs to find its way into your policies, budgets, and priorities. If that is the core of your place brand and what makes your place special, it needs to find its way into everything.

Guides are often seasonal workers. They make all their money in a short season, and then they're either transient and moving around, guide different seasons, or perhaps are servers or bartenders or take on other seasonal jobs in between guiding seasons. That creates unique housing challenges. A community's housing policies that allow for that guide culture require a different approach to housing than they do in the community that doesn't have as much of a transient workforce. Additionally, many guides camp, living in a tent or out of a van during the guide season. What are your policies on where people can camp and where they can park and sleep in their vans? Do they have access to restrooms, showers, water, and electricity?

If guides can't afford to live here and they can't park their vans or camp, then they can't be here. If that happens, it's not that we'll just lose the guides needed to operate our services and support a tourism economy. It's that we'll start to lose our entire culture, everything that makes Salida, Salida. We won't just lose those active guides. We'll lose future generations of past guides that go on to become mayors, city council members, police officers, teachers, construction workers, business owners, and home builders that all have that connection back to guiding and a passion for and connection to Salida. We'll start to lose that and, in turn, will lose the identity of our place.

So yes, what makes your community special probably is the people, but you have to go a lot deeper and have to really understand what exactly it is about the people. That's not easy to do. It takes a lot of listening, a lot of observation, and a lot of piecing it all together. And once you figure it out, the work doesn't stop there. You have to understand what to do with it so that you can protect it, nurture it, and celebrate it so it can continue to be recognized, valued, and invested in. That starts with giving people the words and messaging so they can easily understand it and convey it. When discussions about housing, planning, parking, programming, and budgeting come up, you already have those words and that shared vocabulary.

That is the power of a place brand. It defines those values and gives you the shared messaging for it. If you can't communicate something or clearly define it, it's really hard to protect. Even if everyone knows it's there but they can't quite define it, or they all define it in different ways, it can be challenging. You may very well know that it's a problem that if guides can't afford to live here or have safe access to facilities, the community may not have fully identified that as a core to what makes Salida, Salida. And we could lose it.

It can feel like an ah-ha moment when you give people those words. It will often feel so simple and obvious, and that's when you know you're on to something. That's one of the most important things in place branding: simply giving people the shared words to capture what they already know and already believe. That's how you start to make changes. You can't impact change if people don't have that shared vocabulary and shared words.

As I was writing this book, President Jimmy Carter passed away. Jimmy Carter was an avid fly fisherman. I don't know if he ever fished the Arkansas River here in Salida or not, but there was a powerful quote that I read about him. The book is *Jimmy Carter: Rivers & Dreams*, and the quote by Dr. Carlton Hicks is:

Find a good guide, someone you can trust, who always strives to do the right thing. Someone who will inspire you to try your best, who will show you new things and new ways of doing things, who will admit their own mistakes and help you through yours, and who has an ever-growing wealth of knowledge that they are willing to share. Find someone who will learn from their successes and their failures and inspire you to do the same. Find yourself a good guide. That's the best advice I can give. For me, that person has been Jimmy Carter.

That quote is clearly not just talking about a fly fishing guide. It's talking about a guide in the much bigger sense of the word. When you have a community that's built on that, like we do here in Salida, that's what's at stake. It's not just the guides that are going to get our visitors safely down the river, a novice angler to finally land a fish on the fly, or someone safely off the ski lift and down the mountain. Those things are at stake if guides can't live here, but the greater thing that's at stake is that bigger meaning of guide, which is our entire culture.

Now what about people that aren't guides? How do they see themselves or fit into a community that is built on guide culture? I'm not a guide. I'd argue that in most places that have a strong identity and that are known for something, the public still feels a part of that identity even if they aren't directly involved in it. In Salida, Colorado, you don't have to be a guide to identify with and value what comes from that guide culture. You may still embody getting out there on the river, experiencing the outdoors and laid-back culture and community, and then getting off the river or slopes and relaxing over a beer and live music. So there's still very much that guide culture that you are invited to become a part of whether you actually are a guide yourself or not. That is exactly what guides are great at: inviting people in that are outsiders and welcoming them, teaching them, and ensuring they have a good time.

If we look at famous cities across the country, we'll see similar examples. New York City, known as the city that never sleeps, has that hustle attitude and the saying, "If you can make it here, you can make it anywhere." But even people that aren't hustling to make it on Broadway or down in the financial district have that competitive, hard work and hustle attitude that permeates through all of New York City residents.

Think about Austin, Texas, with its "Keep Austin Weird" saying. Even if you aren't directly involved in Austin's local music or art scene, people in Austin very much embrace that identity of being different and all of the culture that comes along with a community that embraces art, live music, and weirdness.

High Point, North Carolina, is known as the furniture capital of the world, and there is a good chance that most of the furniture in your house was at least shown and discovered by furniture buyers at High Point's Furniture Market before it found its way to the furniture store you bought it from. Twice a year, tens of thousands of people come to High Point for the world's largest trade show for the furniture industry. It's where buyers, designers, retailers, and marketers within the industry come from across the globe. Because of that, High Point is known as the center of the furniture industry.

People that live in High Point certainly recognize the value of the furniture industry and the positive financial impact it brings to the community. They appreciate it and value it, but if the city's identity is so squarely placed on the identity of furniture, what does that mean for everyone else that isn't directly involved in the furniture industry? What is their role in the community, and how are they supposed to find a sense of pride in that?

High Point was struggling from an identity standpoint. Should they embrace their furniture identity because it was the largest industry and risk alienating people that weren't part of that or focus on a new identity and risk turning their backs against the very industry that was still very much alive and had played a vital role in the success and history of the community?

When we unpacked that and did our engagement work, we saw that, yes, there were those that were directly involved in the furniture industry. These were furniture makers and designers, but then there was a whole second and third ring of people that were involved in creative trades that support the furniture industry, and these were your photographers, marketers, and even small businesses like coffee shops, accountants, and restaurants whose customers were in the furniture industry.

So when we were developing the brand strategy for High Point, what we landed on was the idea that it doesn't matter if you're making furniture, but what matters is that you're making *something*. We wanted to celebrate the creator in everyone. Whether you're a barista working at a coffee shop making a latte, whether you're an entrepreneur coming up with a new business idea, or even whether you're a stay-at-home parent who's creating a family, no matter what you're doing in High Point, you're creating something, and by doing that, you are part of a larger system. What we create in High Point changes the world.

That was authentic because so many people in that community already were involved in creating things that were being shipped and seen around the world even though they were not as directly connected to the furniture industry. It was a message that resonated with them. They realized that, yes, I, too, am creative. I'm creating something, and what I'm creating changes the world. It became a place-brand movement around coming together, creating something innovative, and recognizing everyone's contribution no matter what. It became bigger than just furniture.

And so it is the people, but the people are different in every place. What is it about the people in your community? The key to uncovering what it is about your people and then being able to truly benefit your people is deeply engaging the community to truly understand the people, history, and culture. To build a brand that tells an authentic story about the community and one in which the entire community can buy into, it has to be people first. It has to belong to the people and be authentic. It can't be a top-down campaign or external entity attempting to represent the people. It can be led by these top-down entities, but you have to get down on the ground level and do the engagement work that surfaces the brand story in an authentic way. In Part III, we're going to dive deeper into the role of public engagement and how to do that as well as how you can surface these stories and identity. But real quickly, first a note on history and culture.

History is extremely important. It is what has shaped our places, and we need to deeply understand it. However, we have to be really careful that we aren't just looking backward. Even when we are celebrating cultures and history, it is extremely important to do so in a way that is both relevant to the people of today and also uses that history and culture to inspire how a community is moving forward. That is the best way to honor history: to use it in a way that actively shapes your future.

Don't just put it in a history book, in a museum, or in a way that is frankly boring and irrelevant to today's audiences. Today's residents, visitors, and investors, are not interested in history for history's sake. Not everybody is going to be as fascinated by your museums and your history as you may be. That doesn't mean that those things aren't extremely important, but what it does mean is that we need to not just understand them but find ways that we can use those stories and use our history to be relevant for today and push us forward for tomorrow. Doing this can not only make our history more impactful but can help us avoid extinctive language.

This was a lesson learned while engaging with tribal leaders on a place-branding project in Alaska. When discussing the history of Indigenous culture, for example, we need to be careful to avoid extinctive language that describes their culture as something only in the past or how they *used* to be or as people that *once existed*. While their visibility and numbers may have radically decreased, these are often living cultures with real people that are still very much a part of our communities today.

The same thing applies to other cultures, such as an immigrant community, a historically Black neighborhood, or a key industry or trade that shaped the community but has evolved over time. We have to be careful not to present history or a culture as something that is *over*. We need to recognize its ongoing influence and the ways those people and cultures are often still very much present and an active part of the community. We need to ensure that in an effort to highlight the past, we aren't unintentionally erasing those that are still here and actively contributing to a place's story.

Understanding that "it's the people" is only the start. The key to place branding is uncovering what exactly makes the people in your community unique and then using that to shape policy, priorities, and the place itself.

## Profit

For too many places, profit and economic impact is the sole motive and indicator of place-branding success. Profit cannot be the only focus of a place brand. However, it also shouldn't be viewed as a bad word. Profit is vital to ensuring our places are thriving and sustainable, but there is a big difference in profit that benefits the local community and profits that are extractive and benefit outside sources. Without a thriving local economy, communities can't reinvest in infrastructure, public spaces, small businesses, quality of life, or environmental sustainability. Place branding should foster a system where economic growth benefits the local economy, ensuring that success reinforces the place brand rather than using a place brand to extract wealth.

A key to getting this right is understanding where the money goes. If a place brand attracts visitors, businesses, or investors but the income isn't reinvested in the community or, worse, funnels out of the community, it does little to build long-term prosperity.

I'm sure many of you have heard the term "heads in beds." It's often used to describe the goal of many destination marketing efforts to attract visitors (heads) and get them to stay in hotels (beds). However, it is also used to describe, and control, how hotel occupancy tax (HOT) or transient occupancy tax (TOT) can and can't be spent. In many communities, state or local ordinances require that these revenues can only be used for things that directly promote tourism and attract overnight visitors. "Directly" is and should be up for interpretation. A narrow interpretation of hotel occupancy tax funds is problematic because it only allows for additional marketing to attract more visitors over tangible improvements in the place itself that could both benefit the local community and attract visitors.

Many communities are now advocating for broader interpretations and rewriting of these ordinances to allow these funds to be used for infrastructure, beautification, wayfinding, and public amenities that enhance the visitor experience as well as the residents' quality of life. This shift in how places reinvest profits is necessary, and place leaders and legislators need to advocate for it.

Visitors don't just respond to ad campaigns, and they aren't solely drawn to attractions designed only for them. Visitors are drawn to authentic, vibrant, beautiful places, which are the same places that people want to live. It's why when we're on vacation in a beautiful, walkable town, we stop to look at the real estate listings in the window and daydream about living there. Improving a place for locals also improves it for visitors, and the two shouldn't be viewed as separate or competing priorities.

Getting this right is vital for the long-term success and sustainability of communities. If anything, ordinances should state that a percentage has to be reinvested in projects that benefit the local community. That makes more sense than a policy that prohibits it. Why would we impose a policy on ourselves that hurts our local community? Only allowing these funds to go to outside marketing rather than internal improvements is what leads to overtourism instead of making tourism work for and benefit locals.

When cities invest in themselves, that public investment leads to private investment. So it's not just the right thing to do. It makes financial sense. The World Bank published a paper titled "'Crowding In' Effect of Public Investment on Private Investment Revisited," in which they examined the relationship between public and private investment in 109 developing countries from 1980 to 2019. The study showed that for every $1 in public investment, $1.60 in private investment followed. This reinforces the importance of reinvesting funds in actual public investment that aligns with the community's brand values.

When done right, this sends a very strong signal to investors and entrepreneurs that the community has a clear vision for its future. When branding efforts are aligned with sustainable development goals, communities can attract investment that strengthens its local economy, infrastructure, and long-term economic resilience. However, this signal isn't just sent to outside investment. It also inspires confidence from local entrepreneurs and businesses by showing them that your community is a great place to put down roots and to invest.

To maximize the benefits of this economic activity, we need to ensure that money stays within our community. A circular economy is where goods, services, and profits continuously recirculate locally. When you spend money at a locally owned business, that dollar doesn't just stop there. Local businesses are more likely to get supplies from other local vendors, hire local employees, and spend their money and profits locally. That means every dollar spent at a neighborhood coffee shop or independent bookstore circulates multiple times. In contrast, much of what is spent at a national chain is extracted, with profits flowing to corporate headquarters rather than staying in the local economy. A strong local economy isn't just about buying local and benefiting one business. It's about building a system and a local economy that reinforces the identity and long-term sustainability of a place.

It's not just about highlighting unique local businesses, experiences, and products that encourage residents and visitors to support local businesses. Just like your place brand helps you understand what makes your people unique and then influences your policies, your place brand should also shape economic development policies and decisions to favor local businesses and investment.

This makes me think of the first time I visited Juneau, Alaska, while on an Alaskan cruise. While the views and the ship itself were incredible, I couldn't wait to arrive in Juneau and explore the capital city of Alaska. I had seen many photos of downtown Juneau and its combination of historic charm and Indigenous heritage. I was excited to see the architecture of downtown and its weather-worn wooden storefronts mixed with totem poles and formline designs of the Tlingit people.

As we got off the ship, we started hurriedly walking down South Franklin Street as I wanted to make sure we had time to see everything before we were shuffled back onto the ship with the other cruisers. I remember passing a jewelry shop and thinking, *Skip. What's next?* But the next place was also a jewelry shop. *That's two weird jewelry shops right next to each other*, I thought. Next was a cheap souvenir shop then another jewelry shop. *What the heck, a third jewelry shop? Where are the authentic Alaska shops I was hoping for?* The buildings looked like what I had hoped for and expected, but it felt like a bait and switch. It was a false facade of culture filled with jewelry stores looking to capitalize on the thousands of tourists that take over the town during the summer.

While the entire cruise industry has numerous environmental issues, the point I'm making here is the economic case. It's not just hurting the planet. It's hurting the local economy. The vast majority of these jewelry shops are not owned by locals. Local artisans and businesses can't afford to occupy this price of real estate that is driven up by the cruise industry. That's a problem. If viewed through a triple bottom line, this would certainly be flagged and raise concerns that need to be addressed.

A strong place brand doesn't just support individual businesses but rather raises the economic ceiling for all businesses and entities, as discussed in Chapter 3. Economics is all about momentum, and that circulation and reinvestment arms your community with the ability to attract and retain talent, makes your community an easier place to start a business, and creates a stronger local market that can support businesses. This creates an environment where businesses, workers, and entrepreneurs see opportunity and want to stay and invest. A compelling place brand sends a strong signal to skilled professionals, creative thinkers, and innovators that the community values their contributions and offers the resources they need to succeed.

## Place

All of this can feel very contradictory. We're trying to promote places while at the same time preserving and protecting them.

I'm a fly fisherman. I would say most fly fishermen consider themselves to be environmentalists. They typically practice catch and release, are very careful when handling fish, and always keep them wet. We don't fish for cold-water species like trout when water temperatures get above sixty-eight degrees as it causes stress to the fish, and most fly fishermen care deeply about the future of our rivers, oceans, and natural ecosystems.

For those that don't fly fish, I can see how this is a bit confusing. We claim to care so much for the fish, yet at the same time, we are literally stabbing them in the face with a hook and holding them out of the water, even if just for a second, to snap a photo to share with our friends. That seems like quite a contradiction. If we love the fish and the rivers so much, why don't we just leave them alone? Here is how I justify it, at least to myself...

If we truly want to save our planet, our places, our rivers, and the fish, it is going to take a lot more people caring about those things than just those that currently fly fish. I believe that you won't protect something you don't love. Protecting these resources is just going to become more and more challenging as resources are further threatened and as other important issues all compete for our attention and priority.

As much as we love the fish and want to handle them delicately, I believe we need to get more people out there catching fish. We need kids out there on the river. They need to catch a fish. I believe it's fine for them to handle a stocker a little too roughly, squeeze it a little too hard, and maybe even drop it in the dirt as it flops around. We need them to fall in love with it. If they fall in love with it, then they will spend the rest of their lives trying to protect it as well. And it's not just kids. It's everyone - young, old, women, men, Black, white, urban, and rural. The more people we can bring into the outdoors to experience it and have access to it, the greater chance we have of protecting it. It can't become a museum display behind glass. We have to get people out there experiencing it. We have to embrace a little bit of the messiness that comes with that so we can protect it in the long run.

Being able to hold these two seemingly contradictory viewpoints is vital to navigating not just environmental issues but also place branding in general. Place branding and managing cities are full of similar contradictions and challenges, such as welcoming visitors while prioritizing locals, revitalizing neighborhoods while avoiding gentrification, and encouraging economic growth while maintaining affordability. The solution isn't choosing one over the other but finding that delicate balance between the two. I believe that when we view a place brand through a triple bottom line, we're able to more carefully navigate that nuance and find the balance.

Two famous quotes that I think reinforce this idea are "The test of a first-rate intelligence is the ability to hold two opposed ideas in the mind at the same time, and still retain the ability to function." by F. Scott Fitzgerald and "I arise in the morning torn between a desire to save the world and a desire to savor the world. This makes it hard to plan the day." by E. B. White.

One powerful way to help visitors learn about and respect the local culture and natural environment is through visitor pledges. Pledges can serve as both an educational opportunity and commitment, ensuring that travelers understand and respect the unique aspects of the place they are visiting. Pledges can be delivered in many ways. There are humorous reminders about local etiquette, like Aspen's playful pledge with lines such as "I will carve the snow and not the trees" and "I will remain in one piece by leaving the wildlife in peace." There are also initiatives, like Banff's approach, where visitors can get a free, branded reusable water bottle after watching an educational video and taking a short quiz. These pledges and educational efforts can shape the users' experience and impact and create a deeper connection to the place. It's not just about getting visitors to follow rules. It's about getting them to connect with your values and culture. This not only helps preserve the local culture and environment but also leaves visitors with a mindset they can take home with them, inspiring them to be better stewards of their own communities as well.

• • •

Yvon Chouinard, the founder of Patagonia, writes in his book, *Let My People Go Surfing*,

> Who are businesses really responsible to? Their customers? Shareholders? Employees? We would argue that it's none of the above. Fundamentally, businesses are responsible for their resource base. Without a healthy environment there are no shareholders, no employees, no customers and no business.

It's both our natural resources and our built environment that together shape our human habitat and our resource base, which we have to be stewards of.

When evaluating a place brand through the place pillar in the triple bottom line approach, placemaking can be one of our greatest tools. The term "placemaking" has become so widely used that much of what gets called placemaking I wouldn't consider placemaking. Almost anything in the physical space these days can get cast as placemaking. Putting a logo on a sign and placing it in the built environment isn't placemaking. That's a sign. And while signs are important for navigation, gateways, and improving the overall experience, on their own, they aren't placemaking. Placemaking is about intentionally shaping the built environment to reflect your brand's values and principles.

Most community vision statements say something about safety, but many streets are designed in ways that are far from safe, especially for pedestrians and cyclists. If safety is a priority, how are you shaping the built environment to actually be safer? Many cities claim to support local businesses, but how many are really designing their land use, zoning ordinances, and built environment to make it easier for small, local businesses to thrive? Placemaking can be a tool for creating those opportunities, whether it's through temporary pop-up spaces, incubator spaces, breaking up old strip centers into vibrant, multi-tenant spaces for local businesses, or lowering the red tape that only larger entities can maneuver.

Most cities say they are welcoming, but their built environment tells a completely different story. If being welcoming is a core value, then the built environment should reflect that. Are there public gathering spaces? Do bus stops have shelters and seating? Are there places in your community that naturally encourage connection and interaction? A place brand isn't just a tagline or a logo. It's the lived experience of the place itself. If the built environment contradicts the values a community claims to have, then the place brand isn't being fully realized. Placemaking is the reality check that makes sure those values aren't just words on paper but are actually shaping the physical space in ways that make a real impact.

# Chapter 7: The Complexity of Place

Cities are complex. It's my favorite thing about places, but it's also the most challenging. They're living, ever-evolving ecosystems that aren't fully controlled by anyone, regardless of who's in power.

When thinking about the complexity of place and how cities are built, I often draw inspiration from Charles Marohn of Strong Towns, who graciously contributed the foreword to this book. Chuck has a great way of framing cities as "complex adaptive systems." An analogy he often uses to explain this concept is a rainforest.

Chuck explains that traditionally cities functioned much like rainforests. They evolved organically over time. People responded to challenges and opportunities as they came up, and they shaped their surroundings incrementally over time. Their strength was in their ability to change and grow organically.

Chuck then contrasts that with a "complicated system" like a car's engine. These systems are full of intricate parts working together, but they are fragile because if one piece fails, the system doesn't adapt or evolve - it just breaks.

The way development works today is a lot more like the automobile than the rainforest. A neighborhood built only for single-family homes isn't likely to evolve into something more mixed use or dynamic over time. When economic stress comes, these places often stagnate or fail instead of transforming into something new.

Traditional cities are like rainforests in that they are more resilient, adaptive, and able to survive in the face of change. On the contrary, modern developments are often like cornfields. A cornfield might be extremely good at producing corn, but if it faces too much rain or sun, it doesn't adapt into something else - it just fails. This analogy should help us to rethink how we build our communities. Are we creating places that can adapt and thrive like rainforests, or are we planting cornfields that are all the same and easily susceptible to failure?

Understanding this distinction is critical if we want to build places that not only stand the test of time but grow stronger and more vibrant with each passing generation. Chuck Marohn and Strong Towns are leading the way on helping cities understand the financial implications of this, and there is no better place to start to understand that than following them. However, whereas Chuck masterfully dissects the financial implications of this, I want to focus on the role of identity in these complex systems that we call cities.

Places are dynamic. They're evolving and changing regardless of whether they are following a more adaptive, incremental growth or if they are changing rapidly and all at once. Either way, things are complicated, and they are changing. Places are also made up of diverse mixes of people, not just buildings.

We have diverse groups of people with different goals, ideas, visions, pasts, and passions. There are those that are new to a community and those that have been there for generations. There are people that want their community to grow and others that want it to stay the same. Some probably even wish they had a time machine to make it go back to how it used to be. There are those that want progress and a more modern society and those working to preserve their past. You have different races, cultures, politics, and personalities. You have a mix of public and private initiatives, small businesses, large corporations, and organizations, all evolving and shaping their community in different ways.

Even between two people that both want a community to grow, they may have very different visions for what that growth looks like. Some may want things to be more dense and envision a high-tech urban entertainment center, while others may want to continue to grow but maintain their current density and therefore expand and sprawl outward in more of a suburban growth pattern. With all this complexity and diversity, how can a city full of millions or even a town of just hundreds of diverse people have a singular identity?

Think about large cities that despite their size and diversity have extremely strong identities. Places like New York, Paris, or New Orleans may come to mind, and we all know what they represent even without recalling any formal logos or campaigns. Even though places are large, diverse, and complex, they absolutely can and do have an identity. Out of the complexity and divisiveness, there emerges a shared identity and vision.

One of the most common questions we're asked is "How can we possibly have a singular place brand when we have so many different people with different opinions on who we are and where we want to go?" Our clients also often ask, "Does that mean we should cater to the loudest voices or the most popular opinions to find a singular direction?"

To answer those questions, I like to share an example of how Toyota approaches their brand. I often work from my home office and have given this example so many times on client calls and virtual workshops that my kids, who have overheard it hundreds of times, will shout from the other room, "Ugh, here he goes again about Toyota!" I think about this every time I start to explain it. Welp, here I go again...

Toyota serves audiences with very different wants and needs.

There's the pickup truck audience that wants things to be rugged and tough, and you can picture the ads of trucks driving through the mud. Then there's the Prius audience that wants things to be more environmentally friendly, with electric vehicles that may appeal to a more hip or progressive audience. Toyota also has the minivan audience, which prioritizes safety and having enough space to fit their whole family. Then there are also legacy customers that have simply been loyal to Toyota for generations.

With such diversity of users and models, how does Toyota maintain a singular, cohesive brand? Instead of catering to just one audience over another, Toyota builds its brand around shared values that each of those different audiences have. I would argue that for Toyota, that is quality and dependability. Regardless of whether someone buys a pickup truck, a Prius, or a minivan or still drives that old Land Cruiser, they know Toyota vehicles represent quality and dependability, and that's what they are seeking.

While all car brands have similar audience segments and therefore provide different models, each car brand focuses on slightly different brand principles. Even subtle differences result in very different brands. Ford has similar audiences but has built their brand around shared values of dependability and affordability. It's not radically different, but it shapes their brand. Subaru builds their brand around safety and adventure, while Mercedes builds their brand around luxury and innovation. They all have similar audiences that all want different things, just like all cities have diverse groups of people that all want different things. Each car brand and each city can provide something slightly different that speaks to a slightly different set of shared values. People all pretty much want similar things when it comes to the places they want to live. But when cities just follow the boring trope of "live, work, play," that's like a car brand saying their brand offers "wheels, doors, and an engine." Instead, cities need to find the nuanced values that they offer.

A key distinction in understanding the idea of building a brand through shared values is the difference between branding and marketing. This is actually where a lot of people get steered off course. Branding establishes a foundation of shared principles. Marketing, on the other hand, uses those shared principles as a jumping off point to then tailor messages to specific audiences.

Toyota's ads for trucks can showcase them hauling heavy loads through rough terrain and speak directly to that audience's wants and needs. The audience will know it is quality and dependable because they see that it's Toyota. The minivan ads can focus on the safety features and family-oriented conveniences, and that audience will already know that it's going to be dependable and quality because it's Toyota. Toyota has invested in its brand and its products to ensure they consistently live up to that brand promise. The brand becomes a short cut. When you see it's Toyota, you're already thinking of quality and dependability. The brand gives them a head start, and the marketing is now free to speak to the nuance of that audience and close the deal.

Cities are composed of diverse groups with different, sometimes polar opposite, and competing priorities. Just like you have the gas-guzzling truck and the Prius, cities have young people and old people, newcomers and those that have been there forever, and those that want it to grow and those that want it to stay the same. Despite all their differences, these different groups all have at least one thing in common: the place itself. Whether consciously or subconsciously, there's something about the location, culture, history, people, or economy that has drawn individuals to that place. By identifying and surfacing those shared values and brand principles, we can start to home in on, uncover, and create a unified identity that respects its diversity but creates a shared identity and brand.

In any community, you'll find a mix of voices, all with their own priorities and goals. It can feel like they're working in entirely different directions, just like my video of fifty people all trying to surf the same wave, but when a place has a clear purpose and shared vision, it brings everyone together under one identity. It gives them that shared shortcut and jumping off point to then explore their own interests. When people see how their individual efforts contribute to a greater purpose, it creates a sense of unity and civic pride.

## A *civic* brand connects diverse voices through shared values.

A great example of this is a story of President John F. Kennedy visiting NASA in 1962. On his visit, he met with NASA officials and astronauts. This was the President of the United States, and he certainly didn't need to introduce himself, but he went up to each one of them, shook their hand, and said, "I'm Jack Kennedy. What do you do here?" The NASA employees, excited to meet the President, shook his hand and told him all about their specific role and what they were working on. Engineers spoke about propulsion systems, while others described complex calculations for reentry. Then Kennedy came across a janitor, shook his hand, and said, "I'm Jack Kennedy. What do you do here?" and the janitor replied, "I'm helping put a man on the moon."

He wasn't building rockets or planning missions. He was mopping floors and cleaning toilets, but he saw how his role fit into the bigger picture. He knew his contribution mattered, and he was proud of their collective mission.

Not only can we find a shared identity among different audiences and diversity, but I believe this contrast is what makes our cities great. Therefore, the identities that come out of diverse and complex places are actually the strongest.

We had the privilege of working with the City of Santa Fe, New Mexico, and during that project, I was able to sit down with their mayor, Alan Webber, and talk about the idea of conflict and contrast in place branding. The following is an excerpt of our conversation, which was also published, with the mayor's permission, as one of our *Eyes On the Street* podcast episodes.

*Mayor Alan Webber:* Some people want to create a new future. Some people want it to be dynamic. Some people are preservationists. How do you find a mental configuration that when you say it, they go, "Yeah, that's exactly right. How did you know what I was thinking?" And that's the challenge. That's the test of any branding exercise - to not just come close to nailing it but to nail it.

*Ryan Short:* In the research and engagement work we've done here in Santa Fe, we've seen this duality of the importance of the history, the culture, and the past but also the importance of progressing, moving forward, and remaining relevant. How do you do both of those things without one offending the other or one stalling the other? And looking back at Santa Fe's history, one thing that stood out was the idea of contrast. Embracing contrast and almost embracing conflict has kind of been a cultural element of Santa Fe, with the different cultures coming together and how beautiful things came out of that.

*Mayor Alan Webber:* I'm reading a book at the moment called *The Geography of Genius*, and it highlights a bunch of cities around the world in different historic eras that turned out to be places where there were geniuses or that there was a genius, a spirit of creativity. Currently reading about Edinburgh, and one of the things the author's trying to answer is, why would Edinburgh, or why would Athens under Pericles, or why would Florence, why would they become places where the spirit of creativity flourishes in a particular moment for a particular period of time? And to your point, he said about Edinburgh that it was a place where the opposites coexisted. You know, they were pragmatic, as Scots are, but at the same time, they were creative. So they were able to combine what many people would think would be two opposing attributes into a single creative spark.

*Ryan Short:* I think that's true across a number of things, the idea of balance and contrast and how conflict often leads to a greater outcome than just going hard left or hard right. It's the creative tension that happens when things that appear to be opposites end up being able to support each other.

*Mayor Alan Webber:* Forty-seven years ago, I worked in the mayor's office in Portland, Oregon, and the question was, could Portland adapt to change in a way that preserved the livability values of the community? Portland was at a tipping point, and in the early seventies, not just Portland but all of Oregon went through a very intensive planning and development program. And the focus was very clear: how to be the most livable state, the most livable city in America. Livability, however you measure that, was the goal. There was a perceived threat, which is always helpful in terms of rallying people, that the city and the state's livability was at risk due to proliferating freeways, air pollution, sprawl - a whole set of environmental and urban planning issues.

And so if you go back to the 1970s, I think Oregon and Portland did a terrific job of developing the strategy for statewide land use planning, cleaning up the Willamette River, with not building freeways that had been put on the map by Robert Moses back in the fifties and instead investing in light rail and neighborhoods. And there was, by the way, a community engagement piece because the city went so far as to create an Office of Neighborhood Associations so that all the different neighborhood associations in the city could be recognized and worked with on a constructive basis rather than truly on a reactive basis.

*Ryan Short:* What was the impetus of that? Was that more of a top-down leadership recognizing kind of the sprawl and challenges and the threats, and they kind of handed that down, or did that kind of come up as "Hey, this is a thing that everybody's recognizing that we collectively want to change so government should do something about it"?

*Mayor Alan Webber:* Both. There was a statewide movement around environmentalism and sustainability. It ended up electing Governor McCall as the governor, who was very much driven by things like beaches for the people, and the first bottle bill came out of Oregon for statewide land use. Oregon and Hawaii are still the only states, I think, to have statewide land use planning. And then the folks in Portland elected a mayor who was very much part of the neighborhood grassroots lead.

It was that great dichotomy, how to preserve what we love about the city while creating a better future for the city. So it was that we love what we have, but if we just keep doing what we've always been doing, we're going to lose what we have. How do we preserve and protect things that are precious while embracing the need to make changes so we can have a better future?

*Ryan Short:* And do you think that's true for Santa Fe now, the idea of "We love what we have, but if we keep doing business as usual, we won't have those opportunities"?

*Mayor Alan Webber:* Absolutely. There's an old story I told on the campaign trail about a Western. It's a story, so take it with a grain of salt. But according to this story, there was a town that was under attack by the bad guys, and they sent for a new sheriff, a hired gun, and he came to see them and did a survey of the community and came back to the town leaders and said, "Well, if you want everything to stay the same, some things are going to have to change."

*Ryan Short:* That's such a true thing in a lot of different avenues of life and cities.

*Mayor Alan Webber:* I do think if you really want to get the temperature of how people perceive their city, you've got to go out and visit the people and ask them open-ended questions. Be really good listeners of the way people think and talk about their own community. And capture, if you can, some of the nuances. A guy I knew down in Austin had been hired by one of the big box stores for a branding and slogan-writing project. They couldn't get anywhere. They were stumped because all the corporate types and the CEO and everybody, their brains, were way too built with corporate jargon. So they started to interview the cashiers. And they asked cashiers open ended questions like, "What do you think your job is?" You know, the old Harvard Business "What business are you really in?" question. And one of the cashiers gave them a one liner: "Oh, I know what I'm doing here. I'm helping people create a home." And that turned into "Oh, that's exactly right. Thank you very much!" So, you know, out of people who don't overthink it or try to write slogans, the more natural and organic it is, the better it feels, and the more authentic it feels.

*Ryan Short:* That's such a great example in that we don't need to overcomplicate it, and that's why when we approach these projects, it all starts with engagement, which really just means listening to those individuals and residents and stakeholders and just asking them open-ended questions like you just mentioned and looking for those common threads.

*Mayor Alan Webber:* And well, it also calls for clarity. I was asking a summer intern here, who's doing some data analytics for us, as I was going to give the State of the City presentation on Wednesday, "Using your data analytic mind, how would you define victory if you're describing the state of the city? What qualifies as a way of calibrating the state of a city? Is it the unemployment rate? Is it childhood well-being statistics, or is there some overarching if you said to people in Santa Fe, 'What's your definition of victory for living in Santa Fe?', what would they say?"

I don't have a single answer, but I think, as you said, that traditionally, we silo it into "How is parks and rec doing" and "What's going on with the wastewater treatment division?" as opposed to "What are we really trying to achieve?" Jane Jacobs, in *The Death and Life of Great American Cities*, says that the purpose of the city is to provide more choice for more people. So that's her sort of philosophical, meta-level answer - that cities work when they provide more choices for more people. How would Santa Fe stack up in terms of providing more choices of jobs, housing, education, whatever, compared to how it was ten years ago? Are we doing better or worse?

So yes, places are complex, ever-changing, and shaped by an ebb and flow of responsibility and control. However, even in conflict, there can be a shared vision for a place where residents, businesses, and leaders align around a common purpose. That is when a place can become unstoppable. Our places are too important to leave to chance or simply let one voice control.

# A *civic* brand embraces tension as a tool, not a threat.

New York City is a great example of how even the strongest identities come from places of contrast. The greatest cities in the world are really just collections of great neighborhoods. What makes NYC great is its collection of different neighborhoods like SoHo, Chelsea, the Lower East Side, the Upper West Side, Williamsburg, and countless others. Each neighborhood and borough has its own character and culture, but when they come together, they form the identity of New York City. This diversity certainly isn't a weakness or something that detracts from NYC's identity but instead is the very thing that makes New York City what it is.

Additionally, a place's identity isn't frozen in time. Detroit is a great example here. We all know Detroit was once known as the center of the American auto industry, and the city's identity was deeply tied to that. When that industry declined, Detroit struggled, but it has evolved and adapted and today is rebranding itself as a center for art, design, and entrepreneurship. It feels fresh and new but still has a very Detroit vibe that comes from its blue-collar, auto-centric past, which proves that even the most iconic identities are always evolving.

These layers of change and contrast between groups of people, neighborhoods, industries, and time are what give places their identities, so we need to embrace the complexity of place even if it makes our jobs a lot harder.

Understanding what makes up a place brand and how to apply the triple bottom line to make it a place brand for good is just the start. The real work comes from how a place brand is developed, and that is done by deeply engaging the community and co-creating a place brand not just for the community but with the community.

In Part III we'll explore the role of public engagement, how to truly meet people where they are, and how to build a culture of engagement that powers your place brand.

# PART III: PUBLIC ENGAGEMENT

## Chapter 8: The Role of Engagement

As mentioned in the first chapter, Jane Jacobs famously said, "Cities have the capability of providing something for everybody, only because, and only when, they are created by everybody." I share this belief, and therefore public engagement is the cornerstone of our approach to place branding. I believe it is the foundation of what makes a *civic* brand. You can develop a place brand without engagement, but you can't develop a *civic* brand without it.

Very few communities have experience with place branding, but almost all communities have experience with long-range planning efforts, such as master plans and comprehensive plans. Most cities conduct some level of public engagement surrounding those planning projects.

While the role of engagement in shaping those planning efforts is important, it's very different from the role of engagement in developing a *civic* brand. Engagement in a planning project is often a single task or phase of a project. It starts, and then it stops. There are often numerous projects led by different departments and consultants. It's easy for a city to feel like it is doing a lot of engagement yet it's not connected, so it doesn't build toward a culture of engagement.

## A *civic* brand makes engagement a culture, not a task.

Engagement can't be a one-off project, and it can't simply be a task or phase within a project. Some will hear that and assume I'm simply  advocating for a ton of focus groups, surveys, and sticky-dot exercises for every single project and decision a city makes. I'm definitely not. That would be a massive barrier to progress, and communities would spend all their time engaging and planning and never actually accomplish anything.

Engagement work can be challenging and is expensive and inefficient when it has to be started up again after lying dormant in between projects. I have a 1987 Land Cruiser, and when I don't drive it for a long time, it can be hard to start. I have to sit out in the driveway for a long time to warm it up, and on cold mornings, if I haven't driven it in a while, I may dread having to mess with it and take our other car. That just makes it worse because it sits even longer before I drive it again, making it even harder to start the next time. However, during periods when I'm driving it often, it fires right up and is ready to go.

Engagement is about momentum. Momentum is built through consistent actions and efforts, and therefore it needs to cut across everything, including many things that may initially feel distant from branding.

As we dive into engagement in the chapters ahead, many of the examples and lessons may seem only relevant to planning projects, but they matter deeply to place branding. That is because every plan and project contributes to the place brand, and the engagement efforts around those projects contribute to the culture of engagement that are required to create a *civic* brand.

The way a city communicates and engages about parking, road closures, construction projects, ballot initiatives, budget priorities, public art, events, and safety all adds up to shaping the engagement culture and shaping the place.

A note of caution for civic leaders: It is important for leaders to recognize that individual community members and special interest groups will often claim their voice isn't being heard and say the city isn't listening simply because they don't get their way on a single issue. That can create a lot of tension. That doesn't necessarily mean a community is doing a bad job of engagement, and we have to recognize that it is human nature to be upset when we don't get what we want.

Engagement isn't about getting everyone to acknowledge how great of a job you've done at engaging everyone. It's thankless work, and the better job you do, the more people you reach, which means more personalities, more special interests, and more opportunities for someone to be upset.

Engagement is a lot easier when you engage fewer people and only a specific audience. Catering to that small but vocal group can certainly make things feel really smooth, but engagement isn't about making things easy. It's about going to the uncomfortable areas. We need to get comfortable being uncomfortable and recognize that the tension and temperature that can be felt often increase the better things are.

In a community that is doing a lot of great things, there is more pressure, and tension is often greater. This can be confusing and make it easy to lose sight of how things are really going. In a good community, people care. In a bad community, they don't care. In a good community, they show up, complain, and have high expectations, so they continue to push. In a bad community, they don't show up.

Talk to school teachers about the level of parent engagement across different districts and schools. The school with the most parents showing up and complaining is probably a very good and high-performing school.

I've worked with such a wide range of communities in my career that when I see great communities concerned with the engagement tension around certain topics, I often have to remind them that many communities would give anything to be where they are. Their current state, with all its many issues, is many communities' dream state. Having those issues is a massive privilege.

• • •

Public engagement is more than just informing people, and it's more than holding a meeting or conducting a survey. Public engagement should invite people into the process of truly shaping their places. Inviting the public into community-shaping projects that are often nuanced and complex means that a significant part of the public engagement process has to be centered around education. The public can't properly weigh in if they aren't informed on the topic, although that certainly won't stop many from doing so, especially via social media.

Too many communities approach public engagement for important community-shaping projects the same way as they approach distributing information about when the next city council meeting will be. They assume if they are simply making the public aware of it, then they have checked the box in offering the public the opportunity to weigh in and engage.

Historically, most engagement consisted of presenting completed plans to the community. The public wasn't really being asked their opinion, and it was more or less a formality and a matter of showing your work and explaining why you did what you did.

Over time, public engagement in planning and community-shaping projects evolved to a slightly more meaningful approach, where residents were often given a few predetermined options to choose from. This is an approach that still has merit when done correctly and on certain projects but presents a lot of challenges when done incorrectly. On the positive side, it lets the subject matter experts do what they do best and narrow in on viable options and then lets the public weigh in to make slight refinements or final choices. On the negative side, that can be a bit performative if the public isn't involved in driving the overall direction or vision and instead is just making inconsequential decisions at the tail end to make it feel like they had a say in the project details when in reality they didn't. The key here is the community's role and if they are shaping the vision early on or if they are just providing input on small details at the end.

In projects where experts are primarily making technical and engineering decisions, it makes sense for the public to only chime in on personal preferences, like certain aesthetic decisions and feedback around if they would support the funding of that kind of project.

For example, if a city is designing a new bridge, the public doesn't need to weigh in on if the old bridge is structurally sound or engineering decisions for the new bridge and construction phasing. Those are technical decisions that are best left to the experts. However, the public can certainly weigh in on the aesthetics of the bridge to determine if a minimal and functional bridge or a more decorative bridge that serves as a gateway to the community is more appropriate and if they would support the funding of it. In this situation, the consultant team may design a couple of different concepts and present those along with the costs and different road closure impacts for the public to simply make their personal preference known.

In more significant place-shaping projects, like place branding, the public's role should be different. Residents should do more than just chime in with personal opinions at the end of the project. Instead, they should be engaged at the beginning to help shape the strategic foundation of the project. They should drive the values, priorities, and vision for the future. Following that early visioning stage of engagement, it should then become the role of the experts to interpret that input and make the more nuanced strategic decisions that will best bring the community's vision to life. They can then circle back to the public and show them their input was used and get additional feedback on any nuance of their interpretation and proposed solutions.

This approach is almost the reverse of the bridge example. And yet many communities get this wrong by using the same engagement approach they would for a bridge project. Someone decides the need and develops the technical plan and then simply asks the public for input on aesthetics.

For significant community-shaping projects, the public should help shape the core foundation of the plan and then allow experts to work to determine how best to achieve the public's vision. Understanding this sequence and the role the public plays and the subject matter experts play is critical to successful public engagement.

There has been a growing demand for more meaningful and equitable public engagement. While this is a good thing, the terms equity and inclusion have sadly become political footballs, so their importance fluctuates along with the tides of national politics, which naturally trickles down to the local level. When it comes to cities, I'm an optimist in thinking that most working in that space are public servants at heart and fundamentally believe that greater representation and inclusivity are always better. Therefore, I believe there will continue to be a growing focus on equitable public engagement. This is both necessary and exciting, but it introduces new challenges and potential roadblocks to progress.

Usage of the term "equity" has certainly been growing over the years, even though many companies seem to be going back and forth on their stance with diversity, equity, and inclusion due to political tides. Cities, however, have a greater responsibility to ensure their efforts, and especially public engagement, are equitable. Equity has been the theme of conferences, campaigns, purchasing requirements, and strategic initiatives, and several cities have even created equity officers and official equity policies. This is great. However, from what I've seen, the true implementation of equity hasn't kept up with the desire to simply say the word or create a policy that references it. One reason is the polarizing and politicized aspect, which is unfortunate.

As it relates to public engagement, I think a key way that cities are getting it wrong is that they are confusing equity with equality. Many hear equity and think that means "fair and equal." They host public meetings that are open to everyone, and they post online surveys that everyone is invited to take. They assume that this equal access to engage is the same as the equity work required to truly reach people where they are and encourage them to engage in a way that makes them feel heard, respected, and important.

Engagement is hard because it requires significant resources, including translators, facilitators, childcare, transportation, and investment in outreach and relationship building. It takes time to build trust and have nuanced conversations rather than tallying up multiple-choice survey results. Even when leaders say engagement is a priority, the budgets and deadline pressures tell a different story. Equitable engagement can also feel politically risky, which leads many to default to "equal" engagement efforts, such as public meetings and online surveys, because it feels fair and safe. However, this approach doesn't account for real barriers that keep certain voices out, and if we want to build a *civic* brand, we have to meet people where they are.

## A *civic* brand meets people where they are.

Speak to any city leader, staff, or consultant about the challenges they are having in engagement, and I guarantee you'll hear that the problem is not that nobody engages but rather that it's always the same individuals that do. They will likely tell you all the things they've tried to reach different audiences and are a bit stumped as to why it's not working.

There is absolutely nothing wrong with the individuals that are regularly engaging, showing up to town hall, and taking every survey. They have every right to make their voices heard, and we should be glad they do. The problem is that those individuals don't represent the entire community. We need to seek additional voices, not replace those voices.

When you look at the individuals that are the most engaged, it is almost always going to be older residents that own their home. No community is having a hard time reaching older homeowners. That's not because they care more, because they're smarter, or because they're more informed. It's because that audience has more of a direct incentive to engage, often has more time to engage, and is often higher up within their own personal hierarchy of needs, which allows them to engage.

For most people, their home is the largest investment they will make in their lifetime, and property values are often directly impacted by decisions that a city makes. Therefore, it's logical that the average property owner is more invested in what is happening at city hall than your average renter. Other residents that are naturally less engaged may be students, those that are busy working or raising a family, or those that simply prioritize having a social life in between all their other duties and the directions that life is pulling them. In those scenarios, school, work, family, and personal life take priority over engaging in community projects. There's just a lot of other things going on that may feel more important at that time or honestly may just sound more fun than spending your extra time engaging on city projects. So individuals at a phase of life when they do have more time, which is often when we are older and retired, are not surprisingly more willing and free to engage. So while it is almost always older homeowners that are the most engaged, it is actually not as simple as just age and if you own or rent.

To understand why some people engage and others don't, we need to look beyond demographics and property ownership and consider the human psychology behind it. While many have questioned and critiqued Maslow's Hierarchy of Needs, it can still provide a solid lens for helping us think through how to meet people not just where they are physically but where they are emotionally and psychologically. Where we all are from a needs standpoint impacts our willingness and ability to engage, oftentimes more so than demographics and if we own or rent our home.

At the bottom two levels (Physiological and Safety), meeting people where they are means helping them meet these basic needs. At the middle two levels (Love & Belonging and Esteem), meeting people where they are means meeting them within their social circles and showing them that their voice matters. At the top (Self-Actualization), meeting people where they are means engaging in a way that shows people they are being fulfilled by helping their whole community reach its full potential.

The base two levels of the hierarchy of needs is where we find our physiological and safety needs. Physiological needs are physical things like air, water, food, and shelter, and safety includes things like personal security, employment, health, and the security of our property. If people are struggling or simply focused on meeting these base levels of need, then engagement is a luxury. Someone worrying about food, shelter, or personal safety isn't thinking about a twenty-year vision for their community. It doesn't mean they don't care. They just have more pressing needs that they are focused on.

For individuals focusing on those first two levels of needs, it's pretty clear why that is an audience that can be challenging to engage. But that doesn't mean we can't. We've regularly conducted "$5 for 5 minutes" strategies, where we partner with a local grocery store in low-income neighborhoods and literally hand people a five-dollar bill as they are walking into the grocery store.

In Lubbock, Texas, we partnered with United Supermarkets in two lower income neighborhoods to reach and engage these residents that were not represented in any way across all ages and demographics through previous engagement efforts. This project was incredibly impactful for several reasons. First, many of these community members were paying for their groceries with SNAP benefits, so having an extra five dollars as they walked into the store really made their day. Second was simply the fact that we were there making an effort to hear from them. These were individuals that could easily feel forgotten and ignored, and the fact that we were out there helping them meet an immediate need as well as genuinely seeking their thoughts and opinions sent a very strong message. The questions we asked, which were open ended, showed them we were interested in what they had to say, not just how they would vote. We weren't interested in them just being a number. We were genuinely interested in their thoughts and opinions.

Some communities may balk at directly paying someone to engage. However, when you look at total engagement costs and divide it by how many people you reach in a meaningful way, paying five dollars for a solid five minutes with someone is actually really efficient when you consider that many cities will pay $20,000 for a statistically valid survey that only reaches four hundred people. That's over fifty dollars per person.

If someone doesn't have those basic needs met, we need to approach engagement as not just looking for a way to reach them but also looking for an opportunity to help them fulfill that need. Whether it's holding pop-up engagements at food shelters or providing free meals, free childcare, and other basic necessities, this can be an opportunity to meet a need while truly understanding what those individuals want and need from their community.

The next two levels in the hierarchy of needs are where things start to get really interesting from an engagement standpoint and are where I think communities have the biggest opportunity to reach people they aren't currently reaching. This is where we find Love & Belonging, which includes friendship, family, and a sense of connection, and Esteem, which includes self-respect, self-esteem, status, and recognition. People at this level can fly a bit under the radar when it comes to engagement and leave cities and consultants perplexed as to why they can't reach them. On the surface, they seem like they have everything they need to engage, but many communities simply aren't reaching them or motivating them to engage. When we look at the hierarchy of needs, we can start to see why.

We talked a lot in the previous chapters about the impact that our places have on our health, happiness, and sense of community, so even here, three levels up on the hierarchy of needs, there's a lot of people that don't have this need of belonging and community met. In fact, we all probably struggle with this at different times. We may have food, shelter, and even a great job, with all our basic needs met, but if we don't feel like we are part of a community, then we are going to be less likely to engage.

Like my analogy of the river shaping the canyon and the canyon shaping the river, we shouldn't be surprised that the way today's residents engage, or don't engage, is shaped by how we have built our cities and engaged in the past. Unfortunately, many have been excluded from the process because our communities have been designed in ways that make people feel disconnected, and it becomes a snowball effect of disengagement. So the big challenge is realizing that the way we've built our cities is resulting in less engagement. There's certainly not an overnight fix, but just like how we can't blame a user for not knowing if they should push or pull to open a poorly designed door, we can't blame residents for not engaging in a community that has been built for decades in a way that systemically discourages belonging and engagement.

When it comes to esteem, there are a lot of people in our communities that don't feel like their voices matter. They may certainly have ideas and opinions, but they assume nobody listens to them and that their opinions don't matter. Perhaps that's just an individual's self-doubt, but perhaps it's also because historically their input and voice have been ignored. Maybe they've engaged in the past and they haven't seen any follow-through or action, so they feel a bit burned out. Perhaps they've seen the tokenism or box-checking approach to engagement and think, *What's the point?*

Someone looking to meet their esteem needs has shelter, security, safety, and even a sense of community and belonging met, but their need for esteem, especially within the broader community, remains unmet.

These middle two levels are where you'll find individuals that belong to different cultural groups, which is where their sense of community and belonging is being met. They may not engage in the broader community and instead stick to their tight-knit groups, where they feel more comfortable and find that sense of belonging. I've heard it said that Sunday morning is the time of week when our country is most segregated, and that is because when it comes to faith and worship, most people prefer to do so within groups that are most like them. This level of need is also where you find young people that have many of their basic needs met but simply stick to their close friend groups and special interests. Even parents with kids are sticking to their neighborhood groups that consist of other parents with kids and are likely centered around their kids' activities. They have many needs met and likely have their own smaller community that meets the love and belonging and esteem needs, but they stay very much within their tight community. Their sense of belonging is being met within their smaller, tight-knit group, and therefore they don't engage and seek belonging from that broader community-wide standpoint.

This can impact engagement. We all naturally feel more comfortable with groups of people that are like us. So we may not feel comfortable in larger community groups or speaking up at a public workshop, but we do feel very comfortable within our own group with our people. Maybe that's a church group, cultural group, interest group, or group of friends. It can be Spanish speakers, skateboarders, soccer moms, members of the LGBTQ+ community, immigrants, or anyone that simply feels more comfortable within a smaller group of people like themselves or perhaps feels their voice doesn't matter in the greater context because they haven't met that esteem level yet. These groups, especially different races and cultures, recognize when engagement efforts have been made to reach them yet come off in the form of tokenism or simply checking a box.

For example, a community may have the best intentions and recognize they need to hear from more members of the Hispanic population in their community. They believe if they can get more Hispanics to take their survey, they can check that box and be comfortable moving on in the project process. Typical efforts seen in this scenario are ensuring the survey is offered in Spanish, but that rarely sees any meaningful results. That is because the need that isn't being met often isn't a translation issue as much as that esteem or belonging issue. They likely don't feel confident in speaking up or don't see how it benefits them more so than they struggle with a translation. Offering a translation is a great start and should be done but doesn't meet somebody at their real need. It doesn't understand them for who they are and what their unique challenges are. It views them simply as a demographic, and it views them as checking a box so that you can move on with the project. Instead, we need to meet them at the level they are at, and that means tapping into the groups and relationships they already have.

People are smart. They know when they're being asked to speak on behalf of their entire race or are just a box that is being checked. We should be seeking to understand them and asking them to speak as an individual. Engagement strategies need to not be afraid to see people as different races and cultural groups in order to figure out the best ways to reach them and meet them where they are. However, once we do meet them where they are, we need to shift our approach and engage them as an individual. We need to understand what their individual challenges and goals are and unpack how this project impacts them and could benefit them. If we do that and close the loop and circle back (this part is really important!), and show them how their input was used, we can start to build that relationship. We are then contributing to that individual meeting their recognition and esteem level on the hierarchy of needs.

At the highest level is self-actualization. This is where we really have to be, or at least think we are, to truly be comfortable stepping out and engaging at a broader community level, where we are not just engaging in response to things that upset or threaten us but simply because we are wanting to help make our community the best that it can be.

When we think of those that are the most engaged in communities and wonder why it's mostly older homeowners, this is a key reason.

These individuals feel part of a community because they've likely been in the community for a long time and have developed deep community relationships. It's also more likely that their voice has consistently been heard over the years, so they have that belonging and esteem need met when it comes to engagement. They know their voice matters because they've seen firsthand how they have been able to shape their community over the years. They've seen their power in passing or defeating ballot initiatives, getting council members elected or defeated, and shaping policy.

While communities likely aren't struggling to engage individuals at this level, there is still an opportunity to help reshape how these individuals approach engagement. This can be done by framing questions and encouraging them to think not just about their current and personal needs but instead about the community they want to leave behind. If we can frame engagement around legacy building, stewardship, and empathy, we can invite them to consider the experiences of those that may be at very different stages of life from them, such as young families, renters, students, and future generations.

The challenges of engagement are very real, but they can be overcome by truly meeting people where they are. When you do manage to gather diverse input and truly engage your community in an equitable way, you then have a new and sometimes even harder challenge: making sense of the input, finding common ground, and translating it into actionable decisions. In the next chapter, we'll dive into how to make sense of this to avoid falling for the illusion of consensus.

# Chapter 9: The Illusion of Consensus

As we engage our communities in order to build a *civic* brand and shared community vision, there is a natural tendency to want to work toward a feeling of consensus.

When we've done the hard work of reaching people where they are, we end up creating a new challenge: making sense of all of this data and the oftentimes conflicting ideas and viewpoints that have surfaced. We hoped engagement would make the decisions clearer for us, and for many, it seems the more engagement we do, the muddier the water becomes.

Because of this, many communities look to simplify the engagement process and the data they are collecting by prioritizing quantitative data over qualitative data. After all, it's a lot easier to make sense of a winning multiple choice question than it is to make sense of numerous conversations and open-ended responses. However, by doing this, communities begin to view engagement as a system of "voting" rather than as a system of surfacing "viewpoints." This approach oversimplifies the complexity of people and their opinions and also fails to understand the role of data.

Public engagement should be a process of surfacing different viewpoints, not voting, and these viewpoints should guide nuanced decision making rather than blindly following the data, which is often done in a voting approach.

A *civic* brand values viewpoints
over voting.

Quantitative data is great, but relying solely on quantitative data can keep us from developing more nuanced solutions that address a wider range of voices. I view quantitative and qualitative data as two sides of a coin. While they are both very important, I'd argue the qualitative data is where the nuanced opinions, thoughts, and vision come to life, and in place-branding projects, this is where the good stuff is. Through qualitative engagement, you can have those nuanced conversations that are necessary to truly understand opinions that can't be captured in a simple multiple choice survey.

Too often we lean on surveys and prioritize the quantitative results because it is easier for us to point to the data and show that we are implementing what the public wants and can back it up with hard numbers. It's understandable why city leaders prefer this approach, because it shields them from the burden of making hard choices and any potential pushback. It's easier to point to a hard number than it is a summary of conversations. Even when leaders value the conversations, they still want that hard number to point at and use as a shield. Those numbers often create an illusion of consensus.

Public engagement should emphasize the importance of surfacing diverse and nuanced viewpoints. Everyone brings their own unique experiences, values, and perspectives to the table, and we need to understand the depth of their viewpoint, not just their vote.

If survey data shows that eighty percent are against something and twenty percent are for it, you could make a strong case that you should not do it. You could let the data make that decision for you even without knowing what issue we are even talking about. But that twenty percent that share a similar viewpoint should not be dismissed as a "losing vote" simply because they are outnumbered in your survey. First, these individuals may represent a larger segment that has not yet been adequately reached or even taken your survey. Even when surveys have been properly weighted to be representative, they can't capture that nuance. That is because surveys get weighted across things like age, race, income, geographic distribution, and property ownership. The reality is that people's thoughts, opinions, and values are unique and not always tied to their age, race, and ownership status. Weighting surveys can be valuable in determining the likelihood of a bond measure passing, but we've seen time and time again how wrong polls can be, because you can't simply assume that the way a handful of people voted will apply to everyone else that looks like them.

That is because it has more to do with their hierarchy of needs and personal experiences than their age, race, or homeownership status. People are more complex than that, and that survey doesn't give you the time to have a meaningful interaction, educate them on the topics, and find the nuance in their perspective. Additionally, the perspectives of what would be considered a "losing vote" should be explored as it is quite possible it's not a simple for or against, and you could likely craft a solution that still addresses and considers what would have just been viewed as a losing vote. Instead of over-simplified results of for or against, public engagement should strive to surface the different viewpoints represented within those for-votes and against-votes.

The voting and winner-take-all approach may make sense to a lot of people, but we're probably better off viewing public engagement through what can be referred to as a deliberative democracy process. Deliberative democracy places more emphasis on discussion, reasoning, and building consensus as opposed to counting votes. Instead of a simple majority rule, deliberative democracy is built on the idea that decision making should consider diverse and informed perspectives, a key word there being informed.

On housing issues, I've seen both sides of a ballot measure cite they want to keep their town affordable, which is the reason they support their side. One side wants to keep it affordable by increasing density, while the other side wants to keep it affordable by not allowing higher density. Do they actually want the same thing but just don't understand the nuance and impacts of what they are being asked?

One side probably recognizes that increasing density by allowing for accessory dwelling units (ADUs) and encouraging infill development make housing more affordable by increasing supply - basic supply and demand. However, the other side likely has seen other places that are more built up, denser, more walkable, and more urban, and those places are often more expensive. In that case, I'd argue that it's again because of supply and demand and that those places are more desirable and therefore more expensive. Neither is wrong, but there is a lot more nuance to that issue, and clearly more education and dialogue on the topic is needed.

This approach recognizes that people's perspectives are not always black and white and that the most effective outcomes come from a process that educates, encourages dialogue, and surfaces a range of viewpoints. This approach would unpack that twenty percent minority "losing vote" as well as the eighty percent "winning" vote and explore ways to address the concerns and needs of all stakeholders. Through that process, many that would have simply voted on opposite sides may learn something and realize they have the exact same goals as the other side. It's not about making everyone happy. It's about understanding everyone and making sure everyone understands.

To conduct meaningful and equitable engagement, we have to utilize a range of strategies that go beyond surveys and questionnaires, and that includes a balance of traditional and digital engagement that focuses efforts on reaching people where they are both physically and psychologically and then explores the nuance of their viewpoints. We need to allow individuals to express their viewpoints, share personal stories, and engage in dialogue in an inclusive environment, where marginalized voices are actively sought out.

While this approach to engagement serves to surface viewpoints, it does not dissolve leaders and experts of their responsibility of making hard decisions. It's easy to see why many cities are gladly embracing public input if they can then point to the data to make the hard decisions for them. Data-driven decisions make a lot of sense and therefore is a phrase you'll hear a lot, but a more nuanced approach is to be data inspired. Collect the data, but recognize that quantitative and qualitative data are both data then use both sides of that two-sided data coin to inspire your decisions, not to make your decisions for you.

City staff and leadership often face unfair criticism and negativity from the public. In today's world of toxic social media comments and polarized national politics that trickle down to the local level, it has become easier than ever for frustration and negativity to overshadow constructive dialogue. This negative environment puts incredible pressure on elected officials, city staff, and community leaders, who often find themselves caving to the loudest and most disruptive voices and special interests out of sheer exhaustion and self-preservation.

The problem runs deeper than just social media or public pressure. We have inadvertently created a system that trains residents to believe their only avenue for being heard is through the three minutes of public comment at city council meetings. Because of this, many turn to channels like social media, where they aren't limited, to make their voices heard and rally support around their points of view. This singular outlet for public comment at city council meetings encourages residents to only show up and only engage when something is threatening or upsetting them.

Additionally, public comment is not a time for dialogue. Councils sit and "listen" to individuals share what they are passionate about, but by design, there is rarely a direct response or dialogue, and we simply move on to the next person in line. I'm not suggesting we have an hour-long public conversation with everyone that shows up at council, but if we can create a culture of meaningful dialogue and engagement, then when people show up at council, it won't be just because they are mad about something.

Limited opportunities to be heard, lack of education on topics, and amplified negativity lead to reactive policymaking that hurts communities. We need to foster more collaborative communities, where people feel like they are working together, not against each other.

Leadership and subject matter experts still have a job to do. They need to carefully consider the many different viewpoints and then work to craft sustainable solutions. City staff, consultants, developers, and engineers are subject matter experts, or they wouldn't have been hired. They still need to be able to do their work and make the hard decisions and recommendations even when they are viewed as unpopular. Often those unpopular decisions are the most important ones.

Another mistake that I see communities and even public engagement experts regularly make is that they are simply asking the wrong questions. One of the first mistakes is using engagement questions to validate a pre-existing viewpoint, idea, or concept rather than truly uncovering what people want or need. Instead of asking, "What do you want or need?", the questions are framed as "Does this proposal solve your problem?" For example, asking the public, "Should we widen this road?" shifts the burden of solution finding onto the public. People are experts at identifying their goals and challenges but not so much at proposing solutions. And why should they be? The average person isn't an expert on traffic engineering and understanding complex issues like induced demand. This would be like a doctor asking a patient if they thought a proposed surgery would help them with their symptoms. The patient knows how they feel and they can be educated and informed on the surgery and what it does, but they are not the expert on if the surgery proposed is the right option or not.

Take the example of a busy downtown street. If you ask, "Should we widen the road?", many people might say yes, thinking it will reduce traffic and improve flow. But if you instead ask, "What's the goal of this road or downtown?", they might instead say they want a vibrant, walkable street that supports its local businesses. This answer and the solution that would achieve it are very different from the original question and perceived solution of widening the road.

When you frame engagement around challenges, opportunities, and goals rather than skipping ahead to solutions, you gain a clearer understanding of the true needs. This approach prevents the average person from having to make assumptions like believing that widening a road will solve a problem or which side of a housing initiative will actually make their community more affordable. Instead, it addresses the underlying goals and priorities of the community, and then it's on the experts and leaders to figure out how to achieve that and educate the public on why that solution is aligned with their goals.

Users and residents are the experts on their goals, visions, and challenges. Consultants, designers, staff, engineers, and architects should be the experts on designing solutions to help achieve the residents' goals and overcome their challenges. Too often this process gets reversed, and the public is asked to prescribe or support solutions since the experts assume they already know what the goals and problems are. Effective engagement requires each group to play its role: The public defines the goals and challenges, and the experts craft and test solutions.

This is where more qualitative approaches, like observation, interviews, focus groups, and pop-ups, can play an important role by allowing for deeper insights that are necessary to really uncover the needs and vision.

This balanced approach and focus on asking the right questions is where a human-centered design approach can help us ensure we aren't just getting answers but instead are getting the right answers. That starts with asking the right questions.

## A *civic* brand listens before it leads.

Let me give you a silly product design example of how reframing the question can lead to better solutions. Let's say you run a company that is looking to do some engagement and survey work to see if people would buy your new umbrella that you designed. Instead of asking, "Would you buy this umbrella?" or "Do you like this umbrella?", a human-centered design approach would instead take a step back and ask a series of "how might we" questions before even proposing solutions such as an umbrella. "How might we keep people dry?" "How might we notify people it's going to rain?"

This reframing with "how might we" questions might lead to solutions entirely different from the original assumption that we need a tool like an umbrella to keep people dry. In that instance, you already had the idea that umbrellas are what is needed, so you were doing engagement to just validate that and pick which umbrella design would be best. A human-centered design approach may come up with entirely different approaches, like improving weather alerts or designing a new kind of rain jacket. We shouldn't just ask people if they like or support what you're proposing and instead should engage them in better identifying their needs and goals and then work backward from that information to develop expert solutions.

The second big mistake as it relates to asking the wrong questions comes into play when you start to test those solutions. At this stage, the problem comes from focusing on personal taste rather than strategic objectives. For example, when testing design work, avoid asking, "Which do you like?" By the time you are designing and presenting design work, you should have agreed upon strategic objectives. Therefore, when asking about designs, you should ask, "Which design do you think best achieves X?" with X being that agreed upon strategic objective. This ensures feedback is grounded in strategy, not personal preference.

Related to that, public engagement should not be about simply dreaming and wish-granting. Engagement isn't about asking, "Do you want this or want that?" It's about defining the broader vision and also basing it in reality. If you're going to ask if they want something, are you also asking how it will be funded and where it will go? Most people would certainly want a new rec center, but if it means their taxes will go up significantly, there will be a really high fee to use it, or you then won't do another project they care about, they may have a very different answer. Again, this is why some engagement is best left for those more nuanced qualitative engagement methods, where both education, constant reframing, and diving deeper can happen.

We've done engagement all over the country in communities of all sizes and reached people of all ages, backgrounds, and interest groups, and we have noticed an interesting pattern: The longer that someone has been in a community, the more dissatisfied they are with how things are going. Does this mean every community is getting worse? It's more likely that it's not worse but rather it's just changed over time from what they once knew. With those that have been in a community a long time often being the most engaged, this can have a radical impact on engagement results.

If somebody has been in a community for a long time, they're more likely to be a little older, and they probably look a lot more like that demographic we described earlier that is actively showing up and engaging. If they've been there a long time, they're probably also more likely to own their own home. They're also more likely to be higher up in the hierarchy of needs. They want their community to be the best that it can be. Because they've been there a long time, they've seen how it's changed, and it's likely different, for better or worse, than when they first arrived.

All places are changing, and I find it hard to believe that all places are getting worse. We certainly live in turbulent times, with a lot of very real problems and challenges, so I'm not doubting or discounting any of that. There are human rights issues, environmental issues, social issues, and housing issues that make it very hard for us to find that optimism and feel a sense of progress, especially at a national or global level.

Many places are getting better as more communities are becoming safer, more walkable, and more focused on quality of life. That said, most people want their place to be how it was the day they arrived. That may be the day they first moved to town, or if they were born there, it may be how they remember it through their earliest memories, which we often view through rose-colored glasses as we remember the past more fondly than it actually was.

I hear regularly in the town that I currently live in how great it used to be twenty years ago and how things have changed. However, when they talk about how great it was, they are mentally glossing over the fact that downtown was essentially a ghost town of vacant buildings and zero economic opportunity. Multiple studies have proven that we have a very selective memory of the past.

For many, the moment they arrived in a community feels like the pinnacle of that community in their mind. It's human nature to want to be the last one in and then want to freeze time and close the door behind us. We see that in our country with immigration policy. We want to come to a community, and we're okay being new and being invited and welcomed in even though us arriving probably changes the community a bit. We then want to close the door behind us and not let anyone else in after us.

I think the trend that the longer someone has been in a community, the more likely they are to be unhappy about the direction of the community is really important to understand when it comes to making decisions based on that engagement. I don't think it's as simple as just saying we get crankier the older we get, although that doesn't help. These older folks that have been in a community a long time are often the largest group of people that are actively engaging with your community. They are likely driving civic engagement and have contributed a lot over the years to creating what makes that place great. They have done great things and have built the community with their blood, sweat, and tears over the years. They absolutely shouldn't be discounted.

But if they are unhappy with how things are going, does that really mean that the community is on the wrong track? I believe the fact that it happens in every single community of all sizes and all parts of the country most likely means these communities aren't actually getting worse. It's just the perception of that group because they've been there the longest. The community has simply had time to change the most from when they first got there. A person that just arrived a year ago, even if they're in the same age group and same demographic, is going to have a more favorable opinion about where the community is headed. This is another reason why simply weighting survey results by age and demographic isn't always accurate. In this scenario, it is less about age or property ownership and more about how long someone has been in same community.

In public engagement, chasing consensus can lead us down a frustrating path of either trying to get everyone to fully agree (which is nearly impossible) or defaulting to a majority rule approach, where we blindly follow the numbers and the winning vote instead of truly understanding the range of perspectives. When we focus only on consensus, we ignore the nuances and voices that aren't in that majority. Shifting our focus to consent rather than consensus can be a simple but impactful way to ensure that people are heard, that concerns are addressed as best as possible, and that even those that may not fully agree - or may be on the losing side of a vote - can still see their voice considered in the ultimate decisions.

This is how a healthy democracy is supposed to work. Our government wasn't designed for one party or one person to have total control, even though it very much operates in that way today. It was designed so that even a minority party still has a voice and can shape decisions through the House and Senate. Unfortunately, in today's political climate, as soon as one party gains a majority by a single seat or single vote, it turns into a winner-takes-all situation.

If we focus on surfacing viewpoints and truly understanding people rather than viewing them as a single vote, then we can arm our community leaders with the information they need to make the hard choices in a way that benefits everyone. We can free up experts to do what they do best: design solutions that meet the needs and goals of our residents. That is how we live up to the quote by Jane Jacobs and build our cities together.

# Chapter 10: Getting Engagement Right

When most communities kick off a project, they are excited about the engagement phase and make a sincere effort to prioritize it. They genuinely want to engage their community and are looking for a consultant to come in and wow them in the RFP process by showing them their innovative engagement tactics. What they are really looking for is a magic bullet that will help them reach their community and solve their engagement challenges.

I view it as similar to our cultural approach to health and fitness. Everyone wants to be healthy and look and feel good. However, many of us spend more time researching fad diets and weight loss solutions or buying fitness gear than we do simply putting in the hard work of eating better and exercising. We want the shortcut or magic bullet. We may do it for a couple of weeks or until that vacation or special event, and then we stop.

Engagement is the same. Many communities spend more time planning for engagement, investing in software and engagement platforms, looking for "innovative engagement," and talking about engagement in interviews and RFPs than they do actually getting out there and simply doing the hard work of engaging with their communities in a meaningful way.

I get it. Just like exercise and diet, making engagement part of your community's culture is not easy. As with most things, it gets easier with momentum. It's a lot easier to exercise and eat healthy if you're already in a routine of doing so, but starting from zero is tough. The same is true for engagement. If you've actively built relationships, earned trust, and established communication channels, it becomes easier.

Communities can start engagement during a big project, but it can't end there. They need to build off that project and momentum. However, that is easier said than done. There is a lot of nuance to getting that right. Even when you understand the hierarchy of needs and have mastered the idea of surfacing viewpoints, at what point do you need to stop doing engagement and start getting stuff done? What about engagement fatigue? How do you close the loop and follow through? How do you carry engagement from one project to another so that projects feel like they are building toward a unified vision?

To help address these questions and challenges, I want to offer some practical tips that, if kept front of mind, can help you ensure you are getting engagement right.

## Tip 1: Know When to Stop Doing Engagement

That may sound counterintuitive as I just spent the last couple of chapters talking about the need for an ongoing culture of engagement. We can always engage our communities deeper, which is very true. When I say there are times when we need to know when to stop doing engagement, that is because there are times when we have the information, we have the data, and we've surfaced the viewpoints necessary to stop engaging on that topic and start actually making progress in implementing changes and solutions. We have seen many communities fall into the trap of endless engagement with no action.

I've seen it firsthand, even on projects with the very best intentions, where we are so focused on reaching certain engagement metrics that we miss the fact that we may have already learned what we need to learn. At that point, we're now just hitting these metrics so that our report looks good and we can prove that we did a thorough job.

An example that illustrates this and has stuck with me for years came when we were leading engagement for a Comprehensive Plan several years ago. In the same way we kick off many projects, the project team was taking a driving tour of the community. We had all piled in a city van and were seeing the sights and getting familiar with the different neighborhoods as we were brought up to speed on future development projects and issues that we needed to be aware of at various corridors, intersections, and neighborhoods.

We had completed the morning portion of the tour and had just had an amazing lunch at a brand-new restaurant in the hot new area of town. Following lunch, we were to go see a neighborhood and part of town that wasn't doing so well. As we were approaching the neighborhood, it was pointed out to us that the neighborhood we'd be visiting next was a very low-income neighborhood with many dilapidated properties and that it was a food desert.

Just as we were making a turn to head into the neighborhood, we saw a young mother pushing a child in a stroller. The stroller had several full grocery bags hanging off of the handles. It was nearly one hundred degrees outside, and the mom was walking in the street and pushing the stroller up a steep hill. There was no sidewalk, and her stroller loaded up with groceries would be too difficult to push in the grass, which was overgrown and riddled with trash. In fact, given the heat and distance from the grocery store to the neighborhood, it would be extremely difficult for anyone to carry groceries up that hill in that heat even without pushing a child in a stroller. We were informed that this was a fairly regular occurrence and that people are regularly having to make that walk in the street because many in this neighborhood do not have cars. If a household does have a car, they typically just have one, so it's often used by the parent that is at work. Anyone staying at home has to walk to the store.

Seeing this should be all the information a city needs to know. If there is a portion of the population that is living in a food desert and many of them have to walk over a mile to the grocery store that is down a steep hill that has no sidewalk, that alone is enough data and information for them to know what improvements need to be made. No engagement is necessary.

I fully understand there are many challenges when it comes to grading of sidewalks on steep hills and that funding and construction phasing are complex and simply take time. Building sidewalks isn't cheap, and there is a lot that goes into addressing food deserts as cities don't simply open grocery stores. I recognize things aren't always as simple to solve as they may seem.

At the same time, we know there is a very clear problem and that we need to begin addressing it. What we don't need to do is spend extra effort getting people in that neighborhood to take our survey or engage the entire community on this issue to determine if this type of project is a priority or not. However, despite witnessing this scene firsthand, we found ourselves, in the spirit of equitable engagement, making extra effort to make sure we reached this community and this neighborhood.

While there were certainly other topics and issues to engage that community on, all that did was delay progress on implementing a solution for that specific issue. This was a comprehensive plan, so there absolutely were other things that we could and did need to engage that community on, but what I want to point out and remind you of is that observation is a very important and valid part of human-centered design. Therefore, observation is a very important and valid part of data collection and public engagement. We don't need to hit a number of statistically valid survey responses telling us that walking to the grocery store over a mile with no sidewalk in a food desert is a problem in order to have enough data to take action.

## A *civic* brand turns insight into action.

Far too often we focus on survey results or quantitative data as the only "real data" that matters, and just as we discussed in the previous chapter, this is the perfect example of qualitative observational data that very clearly surfaces a viewpoint and need. Qualitative data and data that comes through observation is and should be just as valuable as quantitative data and other metrics where you can more easily make a pretty pie chart. Even if you do need to build quantitative data to support it, you can quickly gather the number of people living in that neighborhood, the distance from the grocery store, and the distance with no sidewalk. These are all quantitative data points that can be gathered in an hour and that are far more important than spending time and effort continuing to try to get individuals in that neighborhood to take your comprehensive plan survey just because we want to hit a number for that neighborhood and demographic. Understanding users' positions within the hierarchy of needs should tell you that it is likely patronizing to focus on getting them to take your surveys rather than simply offering help and moving forward with action.

Lastly, even if we stopped engaging on that topic and immediately decided that was going to be a priority, it should not need to wait a year for the draft of the comprehensive plan to be finalized and adopted for that recommendation to become an actual priority. Things like that should be flagged and immediately prioritized. At the time of writing this book, I had witnessed that mother walking up the street over four years ago, and the last time I checked, that road and sidewalk had still not been addressed. Meanwhile, there have been numerous redevelopment and construction projects across the community and hours of public engagement reaching that community.

## Tip 2: Coordinate Between Projects

Too often public engagement is only a phase within a single project, and as discussed before, each project is often led by different departments and involves different consultants that have different approaches, philosophies, and tools for engagement. When the engagement phase of that project ends, engagement is over, and there is zero engagement until the next project. It then starts over from scratch, with no carryover or follow-through from the previous project. Far too often those projects don't share data, so the next project simply starts from scratch. They define audiences from scratch, ask big-picture questions from scratch, and build relationships from scratch. And then that project is over.

When engagement is truly a culture, each individual project should feel like they are tapping into that existing culture as opposed to feeling like they are starting from square one. One way that can be done is through developing an engagement brand and platform that will serve as an umbrella brand that all engagement for community projects will fall under.

We have done this in multiple communities, and while these

efforts often start from individual projects, we develop a set of tools, including a web portal and project brand architecture, so that future projects can all tap into that, feel connected, and begin to slowly build a culture of engagement. Now when residents see that engagement brand, they know it is a community planning effort where their voice is being sought. As new projects launch, they simply tap into that platform. This provides communities with a platform to continue providing information and updates on previous projects' efforts, which helps not just with new efforts but with showing implementation and progress on previous efforts.

Many communities have multiple planning efforts going on at any one time. They might have a Parks and Rec Master Plan, Facilities Master Plan, and Trails Plan all happening at the same time. Too often the left hand doesn't talk to the right, and these projects are siloed efforts. Like the fire analogy in Chapter 1, when this happens, a community is simply reacting and putting out fires. Giving residents a single place where they can see everything that is going on across different projects and coordinate and share engagement data between those efforts is a huge step forward in making engagement a culture and creating a *civic* brand that unites these projects.

## A *civic* brand unites every project around a shared purpose.

### Tip 3: Limit Over-Surveying

Engagement fatigue is a very real thing. People feel surveyed to death. With multiple projects, there are often multiple surveys going on in the community at any given time. Sometimes this is unavoidable. Different projects do need to reach out and conduct surveys, and they often need different information at different times. However, much more can be done to coordinate internally and share data between surveys, departments, and projects so that we aren't having to ask people the same questions over and over in different surveys.

Additionally, as you follow up and remind people about your surveys, you can use analytics to identify gaps in participation instead of just resending reminders to the same lists over and over. If we know that someone has taken a survey, they shouldn't get the reminder about the survey closing soon. Little things like that can greatly decrease the level of engagement fatigue. Imagine getting messages about multiple surveys on different platforms and then getting reminders about the surveys and getting confused about which survey you already took and which one you didn't. That can be overwhelming, and it can be hard for an individual to keep track of.

The other thing that goes with that is making sure that we're being very clear in communicating what this survey is for. I've seen a number of surveys that might be for a very specific project, but it just comes off as a "community survey." There can be multiple community surveys running at the same time in a community. Get really intentional about identifying what this specific survey is for and how that information is being used. This can really help people understand if they have already taken that survey and if this survey is worth their time.

## Tip 4: Find the Balance

As we talked about in the previous engagement chapters, cities have relied purely on traditional engagement and public meetings for a long time. During the COVID pandemic, many cities were not able to do their typical town halls and public meetings, so consultants really shifted toward digital engagement. Part of this is really positive and a small silver lining. Because of the pandemic, more and more people of all ages became comfortable attending virtual meetings via online platforms than ever before. They were more comfortable filling out digital surveys and using interactive tools.

While more people are comfortable with digital engagement, it's really important that we don't simply go from one hundred percent in-person engagement that alienated certain segments of the population to now going one hundred percent digital engagement that ends up alienating a different segment of the population. Maybe with digital engagement you can reach more people more efficiently and perhaps your audience is now a little younger or more tech savvy, but you're now alienating a different audience. Getting that balance right and understanding when to use digital tools and when to use in-person is really important.

## Tip 5: Empower Local Partners

A cornerstone of our engagement process at CivicBrand starts with identifying and building relationships and partnerships with community organizations. That's because the city doesn't have the reach and the resources to reach everyone in a community for every project. Therefore, if you can build and tap into those relationships, those organizations can spread your message and reach their constituents, their groups, and their followers. Great examples of these are cultural groups, religious institutions, HOAs, apartment complexes, and special interest groups. A benefit of building these relationships is not only to broaden your reach but by also having leaders of those organizations help lead or co-host engagement or simply have the message come directly from them. A message coming from the leader of an organization or group to its members is going to resonate far greater with its members than if it's coming from a consultant or the city itself.

For example, if a city is struggling to reach the Hispanic population within its community, it could certainly make efforts to translate the survey or offer focus groups in Spanish. However, like we talked about in previous chapters on the hierarchy of needs, that likely isn't the true barrier. It's often a matter of awareness, trust, or not feeling like it really matters to them. If the message and call to get involved and engage comes from the leader of a Hispanic church or Hispanic chamber of commerce, that is going to be so much more powerful than a consultant or the city staff member trying to reach and speak to that group.

## Tip 6: Tailor Your Tactics

This one builds off the previous tip. Just as you're defining those different groups and community partners to build relationships with, you also need to utilize different tools and formats for different audiences. Engagement with youth should look different than engagement with senior citizens. Engaging people with young kids probably needs to be at a different time of day than engagement with business owners. We need to look at all the different tools, channels, and formats and match those with our different audiences so that we're meeting people where they are, not just physically, not just emotionally, but with the right tools and the right tactics.

## Tip 7: Acknowledge People's Time

Time is something that we all have a limited amount of, and asking someone to give up their time, even if it's one minute to answer a single question or read a single sentence, can be a big ask in a world that is competing for all our attention and time. Offering small incentives like food, childcare, and transportation can go a long way in making it easier for someone to be willing to commit the time needed to engage. Overcoming those small barriers or simply making it worth their while can go a long way.

Another really important thing is to not forget to publicly thank contributors and elevate their voices in your communication. Don't just say thanks for being here as you greet them but publicly thank and acknowledge them when possible and where appropriate, especially those that participated in focus groups or committees and with partner organizations that helped you in your communication and engagement efforts. Maybe that is publicly in the planning document, on a project website, via social media, with a handwritten thank you note, or simply sending a thank you email. Making sure that they are appreciated for their time and effort can go a long way, especially the next time you need to engage them.

## Tip 8: Make It Fun

Let's throw more parties than public meetings. When we do engagement, we want to always look for ways to add creativity and storytelling and to use design in the process to make it fun. Don't just make it a lecture with boring slides. Make it engaging, get people rolling up their sleeves and working on their community together, and get them talking. Turn a public meeting or a focus group into a social event by adding food and drinks. Make it a community art project or community celebration. Engagement doesn't have to feel serious and contentious, like the three minutes of public comment feel at city council. It can feel a lot more like a social gathering. Conduct engagement or listening sessions at a brewery, or have live music as part of an event.

## Tip 9: Be Transparent About Impact

I've seen so many public engagement sessions where people show up, they offer their input, and then they never hear anything else about the project again. It just goes away, and they don't hear about it or really have to do some digging on the city website or council minutes to find out whatever happened with that project. Always, always, always close the loop, and do so by showing how their input was used and what the next steps are. Be really transparent about timelines. People often get excited about community planning activities. They think things are going to happen tomorrow and may not realize how long things often take. So be sure to manage those expectations up front. If this is for a planning effort that is looking ten or fifteen years out, be sure to explain that.

My sons are both hockey players, and we drive over an hour and a half each way over a mountain pass multiple times a week during hockey season because our town doesn't have a rink or high school team. Therefore, when the town right next door to us had a public meeting about the concept plan for a new recreation site that was going to include an ice rink, my son attended. He was very excited about the potential of an ice rink being built within five minutes of our house. Much later, after attending and actually speaking at the engagement event, he realized that nothing in the concept plan would actually be built for about ten years and that the community didn't have any money for the project. He was pretty let down.

Communities do need to make long-term plans, but clearly communicating those timelines and the purpose of engagement at that early stage is important. In addition to communicating about timelines, it is vital to close the loop and show how input was used to shape the final plans. Part of closing that loop is showing how the input was used, and if something can't be implemented, explain why.

A culture of engagement is what gives a place brand its meaning, but its only when that meaning is embedded into the daily decisions, policies, and experiences that the brand becomes real.

In Part IV we'll explore creating, implementing, and managing a place brand so that the brand goes from strategy to reality.

# PART IV: BRAND IN ACTION

## Chapter 11: Building the Brand

The greatest brands in the world meant nothing on day one. The brand first had to be created then continually implemented over time, either living up to or failing to meet their brand promise. It had to be managed and navigate the ups and downs. Only after consistently living up to their brand promise do brands develop value and meaning.

That is why it can be incredibly difficult to pitch branding concepts. You're having to show how living up to a series of brand promises can infuse meaning and value into the brand that you are pitching over time. If you are developing a brand, pitching a brand, or being pitched a brand, that is an important thing to keep in mind. Nobody will experience the brand the way you are seeing it in a presentation, and that is a good thing. They won't simply read a brand story. They won't see the proposed logo sitting on a white background on a slide deck. They won't see how it naturally influences policy and decisions and shapes the community. Instead, they will experience it in the natural environment through natural messaging, conversation, and lived experiences. Those are things that can be incredibly difficult to convey or imagine. Developing a brand is really a leap of faith, and you have to buy into the implementation more than you have to buy into any design elements.

When we first start a place-branding project, we start by engaging the community and are often asking them really broad, open-ended questions like "What makes this place great?" "How would you describe this place in three words?" "How would you describe your community?" As we are asking these questions, one of the most common questions they ask us back is "Are you asking about how we are now or how we'd like to be?"

That's because people are often thinking about the future, and there often is a level of aspiration and optimism that they're excited about. They've recognized that their community isn't reaching its full potential or that the story and narrative that's out there about their community doesn't fully capture what the community has to offer. That's typically why we are there. So they are naturally wondering, are we asking how it is now or how they want it to be in the future?

The way I like to respond to that is that a brand needs to be rooted but also reaching. We need to first get very real and honest about all the good, the bad, and the ugly about where a community is now. We need to understand the history, the perception, and everything about where the community actually is. But again, a brand isn't just about perception. It's not about just holding a mirror up to a community and saying our brand is what we are.

So there is a level of aspiration in a brand, but it can't be too far out. It can't be unrealistic. It can't be just a pipe dream. That's when you'll get the critiques of branding and marketing as "lipstick on a pig" or just a fake version of a community, designed to appeal to visitors or investors.

A brand needs to be authentic yet aspirational. The example I like to give people to drive that point home is to think about a time you were out clothes shopping. You're at the mall or boutique shop, and you try on a new outfit. It's a brand-new outfit and maybe even something a little different than you wear every day. But when you put it on, it just feels right. It's new, but it feels like you. And you say, "This is me. This makes me feel like the best version of myself."

Now, it's not a costume. You're not changing who you are. You're not looking to reinvent yourself. You just found something that made you feel like the best version of yourself. It was authentic, it felt like your style and your personality, but it was reaching - just enough. It was fresh enough. It felt good and gave you a bit of pep in your step. It made you hold your head a little bit higher and feel good about yourself.

It's rooted, but it should absolutely be reaching. It's an honest representation of who we are but guides us where we're headed. It's where we want to go, and it serves as that visual reminder in our daily decision making of where we're headed and the decisions we need to make to get there.

## A *civic* brand reflects authenticity and aspiration.

As you start to build brand assets, it's going to be very tempting to get hyper-focused on the symbols that you create - the logos, the words, the colors. It will be tempting to try to capture everything about your community and have it be fully represented in those symbols. But that is a big trap and an area where communities get it wrong.

Your symbols and logos need to be just that - symbols. They need to simply remind somebody of your brand, not communicate the depth of your brand. In the introduction, you may recall we talked about how religions are actually good examples of brands. Think of any symbol from any religion. The cross doesn't capture everything about Christianity. It's a simple reminder so that when Christians see it or wear a cross, they are reminded and inspired, and it shapes their actions.

There are some things that make better symbols than others. I like to think of design as a vessel. Look for a design or symbol that is the best vessel to hold your story and carry your message. Other times it may be helpful to think of it more as a stage or a platform. What symbols, messages, designs, and colors can support the many different stories that you're going to want to tell and the different channels that you'll need to tell them on?

The key is that good branding is symbolic, not exhaustive. The goal is not for someone to see your message or see your mark and instantly understand everything about your community. If you set that as the bar you're trying to hit, you're setting yourself up for failure. At the start of all projects, we ask stakeholders how they will personally measure the success of the project. Many people will say that when they see that the end deliverables fully capture the spirit of the community, then that will be success. Communities are complex, vibrant, dynamic places full of so many different things, people, ideas, and stories that a single mark on its own capturing everything about a place is really difficult, if not impossible, to do. In that situation, you're either setting yourself up for failure and won't be able to achieve that or you're going to create something where you've attempted to cram every single thought and idea about your community into a single mark to the point where the outcome is probably pretty terrible.

I definitely won't mention this city by name, but there's a community logo that comes to mind when I think of probably the worst city logo I've ever seen. What makes it so bad is that you can very clearly see in a single logo about seven different ideas. It was probably designed by committee, and they kept tinkering away on it until every voice and idea was captured and crammed into the logo. The outcome is really problematic. So that logo, the message, and the different elements that you're creating around your brand need to simply be symbols.

Another example I like to use to illustrate that is the lesson that we learned from Pavlov's dogs. I'm sure this is a story that we're all familiar with, and the simplified version is that Pavlov, every time he would feed his dogs, would ring a bell and then feed his dogs. Over time those dogs started to associate the sound of the bell with getting fed, and they would begin to salivate when they heard the bell ring.

What does that have to do with branding? Well, one, the sound of a bell is simply a good symbol because it's a good vessel or stage for that message. The sound of a bell has nothing to do with eating. We may think of that now because of our own association with a dinner bell, but there is nothing inherent in the sound of a bell that has anything to do with eating, just as there is nothing inherent in two lines in the shape of a cross that has anything to do with religion.

It's the repeated association with a symbol that gives it meaning over time. The first time the bell rang, it meant nothing to the dogs. The first time someone saw a cross, it meant nothing. It's only after the repeated association that those things start to take on meaning.

A bell is a good vessel because it's simple, it's clear, and it's not going to be confused with other sounds.

When you think about your community and its internal audiences, you need a simple symbol that can be a vessel and take on the complex meaning of your community as well as serve as the reminder of what your community is about.

These symbols also serve a role for external audiences. A lot in the branding world has been written about pirate flags. Some of it's true, and I imagine a good amount is also fiction, but the lesson still holds weight. As pirate ships approached other ships and raised their flag, there often wasn't even a fight. That's because that flag served as a symbol that in the past had been closely associated with action. They lived up to their pirate brand promise. So now when they raised the flag, people knew what they were in for, knew they meant business, and often didn't even put up a fight. Their action had so consistently been associated with their symbol, the flag, that over time they didn't even have to fight. The flag now carried the weight and did their work for them.

The important thing across all these examples is that your symbols can't be disconnected from action. They need to show up. That is why the simplest marks are often the most impactful. Even in complex brand architectures, those symbols can show up consistently across all channels, from the built environment to your digital channels and everywhere in between.

When your symbols can clearly show up alongside your message, especially when it's being backed up by action, it begins to develop meaning. Over time it can build that connection and will have deep meaning, both internally and externally. If your symbols don't show up alongside your actions or there's no action behind your symbols, you will never create that meaning.

• • •

A great brand doesn't just have a single message that people are forced to memorize or read off of rigid scripts. Instead, we want people to understand our message and our story, but we want them to share it in their own ways and in their own words.

# A *civic* brand creates a shared language.

This is more important with place and community branding than it is with product and commercial branding. In product branding and company branding, you may want to have really tight brand guidelines and strict usage of taglines and messaging. In place branding, we're less interested in that control, and we're more interested in the understanding and the depth behind the message.

So we may write a brand story, we may write a tagline, but we view it as more of a platform, a jumping off point for people to share their own versions of that in their own ways. We start from the inside out and ensure the message resonates with locals and stakeholders. We arm them with the words and the tools to say what they've been thinking and feeling all along, but we now give them the direction and clarity to go say it in their own way. Instead of saying, "Take these words and repeat them," we say, "Take these words, let them inspire you, and go share your own version."

An example of this that I'm actively working on while writing this book is for a place-branding project for the Mat-Su, Alaska. That stands for the Matanuska-Susitna Borough, which is a huge region between Anchorage and Denali National Park. As we were developing the brand and the message for the Mat-Su, we definitely landed on some storylines around how this region of Alaska is ideally situated to allow people that come to Alaska to do *Alaska, on your terms.*

Alaska is a really big place and can be a challenging place to visit. For many it's a once-in-a-lifetime bucket list place to visit, and because it's so big and there's so much to do, it can be overwhelming. Because of this, a lot of people that visit Alaska are naturally drawn to the cruises and the guided tours, or they work off of a checklist of the top ten must-see things to do in Alaska. It's understandable why they do that. There is so much to consider and they may only have one chance to get it right, so they default to the curated and overly guided experience.

But the best way to really experience Alaska is not from a cruise, a guided tour, or even the top ten checklist. The best way to visit Alaska is to get off the beaten path, to get away from the crowds, and to experience it *on your terms* and in a way that gives you the time to pause, slow down, and experience the culture and the land. That's the best way to visit Alaska, and the Mat-Su, given its location, accessibility, amenities, and independent culture, is uniquely situated to allow people to explore Alaska in that way.

Because our approach is always locals first, the brand strategy was centered around the idea of making tourism work for locals *on their terms*, and we paired that message with showing how visitors can do Alaska on their terms. So when we were producing a video for the Mat-Su to highlight the brand strategy, we wanted to speak with different business owners, tribal leaders, and residents so they could tell their story and what it means for tourism to work for locals on their terms. We wanted to interview them and have them tell that story. However, we didn't just give them lines to regurgitate back to us. Instead, we just asked them questions that spoke to that story. Instead of saying, "In the Mat-Su you can do Alaska on your terms," we instead would ask them questions like "Why are people drawn to Alaska?" "Tell me why planning a trip to Alaska can be overwhelming." "Speak to me about how the Mat-Su is uniquely situated to allow people to experience the real Alaska." "What does it mean for tourism to benefit locals?"

By guiding them through our questions rather than feeding them lines, we were able to weave a consistent narrative that was in their own words. This made the message so much more powerful and authentic because we had multiple people saying similar things but all in their own way and with their own unique points.

So when we get asked if the goal of this project is to create a tagline, we always say no. Instead, it's about developing a messaging framework. We want to have strategy in the messaging, but the way that messaging comes out, we want it to happen in one hundred different ways. If you come up with just a single tagline, you're going to exhaust that tagline, and you're going to have to come up with a new tagline pretty quickly. But with a messaging framework, you give people a chance to use their own words and give the message a much longer shelf life and a more valuable and effective way to say something.

To summarize, as you're creating the brand, it's important to remember that it needs to be rooted in who you are but still reaching. The logos and symbols you create need to be just that, symbols, not the sum of everything that your brand stands for. People need to understand your brand vision and story, but don't strive for full control of your messaging. Instead, let your messaging inspire your community in a way that invites them to share the message in their own words. If you do those things right, then you will give your brand a better chance of evolving and showing up alongside that action. That's where you can go from creating a brand to truly living the brand, which we'll talk about in the next chapter.

# Chapter 12: Living the Brand

A brand means nothing until you implement it and are truly living it. Living the brand means you bring that identity to life through action and experience that are embedded into everyday decisions and the culture within your community. It's not a campaign, and it's not just something you say. It's something that you do and that is backed up with action. That is what makes a brand real. It's not running the ad, and it's not refreshing a website. It's not putting up the new signage.

Those are the symbols and reminders of the brand, but they're not what gives the brand meaning and not what makes it real. What makes the brand real and allows you to truly live the brand is implementing it through small things, in daily decisions, and by having your community adopt the brand by using it in their actions as well.

## A *civic* brand shows up in everyday decisions.

## The Small Things

Too often communities focus on big things and lose sight of the value of multiple small things. One of my favorite stories of a community living the brand is from Jason Thorne. Jason appeared on our podcast, *Eyes On The Street*, in the episode called "Living the Brand." At the time, Jason was with the City of Hamilton, Ontario, and he's now chief planner for the City of Toronto.

In that podcast episode, Jason shares with us how Hamilton, Ontario, wanted to be known as a music city. That's what they felt they were and were striving to truly be. Now, they could have focused on really big things, like holding a massive music festival, or they could have spent millions of dollars on a huge music hall. They could have done a lot of big things, but what they did instead was focus on the small things. They asked themselves, "What small things can we do to truly be a music city and truly live that brand?"

They engaged with their community and surfaced problems and challenges in areas where they weren't living up to truly being a good music city, with the goal of finding small ways to change that. Through this process, they came up with some really great things, such as implementing musician loading zones. Can you really be a music city if a drummer is going to get a parking ticket or have a hard time loading his drums into a venue? With musician loading zones in front of venues, it sends a visible signal that you value musicians, and you take one more real step toward living the brand of being a music city. That's something that can only be surfaced through engagement and human-centered design. By observing and listening to discover where the challenges are, you can then begin to design ways to overcome those challenges.

They also looked at their busking laws. Can you really be considered a music city if you're going to be running musicians off your streets or giving them tickets? They then looked at permitting music on patios. Can you really be considered a music city if places can't have music on their patios? When you picture walking down the street of a music city, you're certainly expecting to hear some music.

You have to first do the work to figure out what it is that you're trying to be, and then you have to go through that engagement and human-centered design process to surface those challenges that keep you from achieving it. When you do that, you will inevitably surface small things that you can do to live the brand. We always recommend prioritizing those small things over the big things because one hundred small things that say you're in a music city are going to go a lot further than just one big thing. What are the small things that come to mind for your community?

## Daily Decisions

The second part of living the brand is infusing it into daily decisions. Whether that's the decision making of council, leadership, developers, residents, or business owners, it needs to be part of everyone's decision-making process.

Think about how communities are planned and decisions are made. You hear a lot about master plans, and we've worked on a number of them over the years. There's a type of master plan that I like, and there's a type of master plan that I don't care too much for. The type of master plan that I don't like is one where you're literally making every future decision. You are master planning where every brick is going to go, and you are making a series of future decisions that people are just going to implement and follow. The reason I don't like that is because it's not realistic.

Think about your plan for life and how your plans have changed over the years. Some people, at a very young age, may say they want to go to a certain school, want to graduate in a set number of years, want to get married by a certain age, and want to have two and a half kids by a certain age. They may have all of these things in the game of life perfectly planned out, but that's not how life works. You don't know the challenges or opportunities you are going to face along the way. As much as we may want to, nobody can truly master plan their life.

Now, we certainly can and should have plans and a vision rather than drifting aimlessly. What typically happens is you have core values, beliefs, and goals about where you're headed and where you want to go. You use those values and beliefs to make daily decisions. You may hope to get married by a certain age and you may hope to have a certain number of kids, but that may or may not be in the cards. Instead, you have to make decisions that you believe will lead you where you want to go and will tee you up for success.

Cities and communities are the same. A good example of this comes from the work we did on an Open Space & Trails Master Plan for Breckenridge, Colorado. A primary reason they needed to do a new master plan was because their old master plan didn't address many of the congestion issues they were now facing. More and more people wanted to get outside and find space in response to the COVID pandemic, and more and more people were looking to escape summer heat in hotter states and come to Colorado, where it's much cooler in the summer, and hit trails. They needed a new master plan that addressed many of the challenges that came from that increased pressure, congestion, and conflict.

The problem is, you can't plan for unknown things. You can't plan for a pandemic. You can assume that there are going to be more pandemics in the future, but you don't know exactly what they're going to look like and how they may impact you. Will the next pandemic put even more people on our trails, or will it decimate tourism?

With the new master plan for Breckenridge, we helped them focus on not making all of their future decisions, such as where exactly new trail connections need to be made, exactly what properties to acquire, or which trails should be directional versus one way. Instead, we helped them develop decision-making principles that will guide them on how to make those decisions when they get to them in the future. The master plan was more of a decision-making framework. That's what a brand is and needs to be for a community - a decision-making framework.

Decisions are going to have to be made on things that we can't predict or even imagine today. We can't prescribe answers to unknown challenges, but we can arm a community with the principles to make those decisions. Therefore, a significant part of a brand is its brand principles, which should be used as decision-making filters in every decision that is made, from big decisions to little decisions. From deciding which photo best represents the community to shaping zoning policy, a brand principle can and should influence both of those.

Brand principles are unique to every community, but the part that's not unique to every community is that triple bottom line. Communities should use both their brand principles and the triple bottom line as a lens to view decisions through. Ask yourself, "How does this decision relate to our brand principles, and what does it mean for our people? How does it impact our prosperity? What does it mean for our place?" Both the principles and triple bottom line become decision-making filters for helping us live the brand and act on it on a day-to-day basis.

Those brand symbols that we create, the messaging and logos, become our reminders of our branding principles. The logo on the wall in council chambers, on the welcome sign, under our email signatures, in murals, on street banners, and on our website and social media aren't just decorating and promoting. They are there to remind us of our responsibility to infuse those brand values into our daily decision making. This is why they are just as important, if not more important, for local and internal stakeholders than they are for visitors and external audiences.

## Community Adoption

The third way to truly live the brand is to make implementing the brand a community task, not just a task for one organization or entity to do alone. For the brand to be successful, it has to essentially go viral within your community. It has to be adopted, shared, repackaged, and remixed by your community members, your residents, your visitors, and your business owners. To do that, you need to give them tools, not just rules. As branders, we naturally love rules and want to control a brand, but in place branding, we need to focus a little less on the rules and more on tools. What are the templates, brand kits, and storytelling guidelines that we can give our community? What are the ways we can package our message that get people excited and want to share it?

Maybe that's a "made-in brand" that a business owner can tap into and use to share in their business and on their packaging. It can be a brand or marketing toolkit that people can utilize, or it can simply be shared language and shared messaging that people can riff off of. In our work with the Mat-Su, Alaska, we gave them the idea behind the message, and that inspired them to tell it in their own way. We simply amplified their message.

• • •

One of the first lessons I learned in place branding was the value in giving people the tools and language to share a positive message. It was 2008, and we had just started our company. As I'm sure many of you recall, 2008 was right in the middle of what would become known as the Great Recession. It was certainly an interesting time to be starting a company. My wife and I were expecting our first child, and I had just quit what was, at the time, the highest-paying job I had ever had in order to start a company that had no clients. She was about to be out on maternity for at least a few months, and we blissfully thought, *Maybe we should quit our jobs and start a company.* Looking back seventeen years later, it was indeed the perfect time to start our company and the right decision for us, but it definitely took a bit of blissful ignorance to make that leap.

As the country was heading full steam into a recession, one of the first projects we worked on was one that, in hindsight, really set the stage for how we approach place branding, even though at the time, we didn't use that term or even think of ourselves as a place-branding agency. It would take us a few more years to understand what that even meant and have the courage to narrow our focus because at the time, we were simply designers and marketers looking to help tell the story of any business that would hire us.

The project was the Texaplex, which we took on for one of our clients, David Winans. David was a real estate broker, and this was sort of a side project that he asked us to help with outside of marketing his real estate company. "Texaplex" was a term that David coined to describe what others may know as the Texas Triangle. It is the triangular region in Texas that is where eighty percent of the population lives. It is made up of Dallas/Fort Worth at the top, down to Houston, over to San Antonio, and then starting back up toward Austin to finish out the triangle. So while Texas is a massive place, most of the people, development, and growth are all within this region.

Recessions often get exaggerated and made worse by a snowball effect as the doom and gloom of recession talk dominates the news and conversation, which in turn lowers consumer confidence, slows spending, and slows hiring and then makes the recession even worse. It's not unlike the faux gas and toilet paper shortages, where simply the rumor of a shortage results in an actual shortage because everyone rushes to the pump and is driving around with a full tank of gas and closet full of toilet paper. It manifests itself, and there becomes an actual shortage or recession.

While it was very much a legitimate recession, and at the time the most severe financial and economic meltdown since the Great Depression, things within the Texaplex actually weren't quite as bad off as the rest of the country or at least as bad as the media made it seem. The entire point of the Texaplex project was to spread the good news in an effort to combat the bad news. Being in real estate, David was of course interested in telling the good news of Texas so that his agents remained hopeful and people would continue to buy and sell homes with confidence. Yes, we were headed into a recession, but those in the Texaplex were quite fortunate, and a lot of things just weren't as bad as they seemed.

The Texaplex project was simply a seven-minute video and honestly really just a glorified PowerPoint with a voiceover, but the production value didn't matter. What mattered was that it spread the good news, tapped into people's sense of pride, and did so in a way that was easily shareable. The video went relatively viral for the time, specifically within certain industries. Businesses started sharing the video and using it within their own marketing to promote their own businesses. Many high-profile entities, organizations, and individuals were sharing that message. It was an infectious message because it was all about telling the good news of a place that people called home.

If you get nothing more out of this book, know that people want something to be proud of, even in hard times, and if you give them the tools to share their civic pride in a way that is authentic and can benefit them, they will proudly do so.

## A *civic* brand helps people share what they love.

Every place has its challenges, but there is always a positive story to tell. That said, place branding and marketing aren't about creating a false version of your community just to attract visitors or outside investment. Unfortunately, a lot of communities do that. Instead of making actual improvements and shaping their place, they just shape the message and make no real impact on the place. When residents hear about a branding effort in their city, it makes sense that they assume it's just going to be a marketing spin and a waste of money because that is often what many cities do.

The Texaplex project wasn't really a place-branding or economic development project at all. We simply set out to spread some positive news. The video shared interesting and entertaining facts about the growth, size, and opportunity of the region. As the video was shared, it got credited for playing a role in some significant economic development wins, even if it was just one small piece of the puzzle. The Texaplex project actually got some credit as one of the reasons Toyota moved its headquarters to the Dallas/Fort Worth area. It certainly was not *the* reason, but the video captured and packaged many of the actual reasons in an easily shareable and digestible format. It was told to us that the Texaplex video had made significant rounds within the Toyota leadership team, to the point where the CEO half-jokingly said, "If one more person sends me this Texaplex video!"

The governor of Texas also played the video for people around the world on economic development trips, and when you went to his office, the video was on repeat in the reception area. The governor actually requested a meeting with David and me to simply thank us for creating the video.

It wasn't just the big examples, like Toyota and the governor, that proved the value of this type of storytelling. Literally thousands of realtors and hundreds of chambers of commerce and businesses all across the state and the country were taking the Texaplex video and sharing it. The video was originally meant to be an internal project to inspire David's team of real estate agents, so we didn't have any budget to push it out there and get it in front of people. But that didn't matter. People found the video and forwarded it to colleagues, shared it on social media, and embedded it on their own websites. A few even stole it and added their own logo to it. They shared it to share their civic pride for their home state, they shared it as a tool to help market their businesses, and they shared it because they, too, believed that spreading the good news was the best way that they could combat the recession.

That was a really valuable early lesson, not just about sharing the good news about a place but about creating an asset and narrative that others can latch on to and easily share alongside their own brand and message. Aside from the few that stole it and added their logo, this allowed others to use it and freely share it and embed it without worrying about copyright or feeling like they were just sharing a commercial for a real estate company. Most clients would have put their logo and a copyright all over it, but David very intentionally didn't. The goal wasn't for it to be a marketing tool for his business but rather something people would willingly share. He wanted to first send an inspirational message to his agents and their clients and second put that message out there to the world. He knew nobody would share it if it came off as a commercial for his company.

By making a video easily shareable and packaged in a way that can also benefit your audience, you're helping them achieve their own goals as well as aligning the community on a shared message that gets amplified to the world. This approach is a lesson we carry forward into every project that we do, whether it's developing a "made-in brand" strategy or creating tools, templates, and assets that businesses can utilize in their own marketing that benefit their business while at the same time amplifying the place brand. This is a win for the place and a win for the individual.

• • •

When a community gets to that point where they're looking to roll out a brand, they're often looking to do a big brand launch, throw a big party, and celebrate the hard work that everybody's put into it. That's understandable, but that doesn't make sense to do in every community.

In many places, I'm a big fan of the soft launch. A soft launch is really valuable when there's an element of your brand where you have to earn it before you can say it. There is an aspirational element, that North Star, and you have to make some positive steps forward of earning it and living it first. By soft launching your brand strategy, you give yourself the opportunity to make some of those brand-based decisions, run some things through your brand principles, and get some quick wins by implementing some of those small things. If they're done correctly and your brand is associated with those actions, then you start to earn the brand. By soft launching it through those efforts, you're not just saying, "Here's our new brand! Look at us!" All that does is invite your critics to say that's a fake version, that it's just for visitors, or it's lipstick on a pig. You may not have earned it yet, so they may be right.

This slow rollout can also make it feel natural and like it's just been there all along. A story that I love about soft launching a brand and it feeling like it's been there all along is from a project we did in Park Rapids, Minnesota.

We were hired by the Park Rapids Lakes Area Chamber of Commerce, which is a bit of a mouthful of a name. The reason it was called that was because it wasn't just Park Rapids. It was an area and community that also consisted of Akeley, Menahga, Osage, Nevis, Dorset, and Lake George. They were looking to create a brand that could represent the whole area to help them extend their shoulder seasons and attract talent to their communities. When we did our engagement and we started talking to people in those different communities, the second you said, "Park Rapids," they were out. They loved Park Rapids, and it's certainly the most known town in the community and the center of the region, but they weren't Park Rapids. "We're Osage. We're not Park Rapids." "We're Menahga, not Park Rapids." They knew that their message and the story of the area as a whole was better and stronger together, but that name just didn't work for them. Through our engagement and branding process, we developed Heartland Lakes as a new name to define the region. And I've got to tell you, I was incredibly nervous because coming up with a brand-new name for a region that people have visited for years and that many have called home for generations is quite daunting. Are people going to buy into it? How do you just fabricate a new name for a place?

Because we did it the right way, through meaningful public engagement and the development of core brand principles that were used to slowly soft launch and earn it over time, it has been embraced. It's been eight years since we started that project, and there is now even a public charter school in the area named Heartland Lakes Community School, and businesses such as Heartland Lakes Self Storage have been created. The community has really adopted it. In fact, in some follow-up engagement, we've even asked about the name and have heard some people say that the area has always been called Heartland Lakes. That's when you know you've nailed it: when it doesn't even feel like a new thing and people assume it's been called that all along. It was able to slowly and naturally become part of the vernacular. We didn't force it on anybody, and now there are people, even people that have lived there a long time, that buy into the name. Some of them even feel like it's been called that their whole life!

Living the brand is a coordinated process of internal alignment, external rollout, and very intentional storytelling. It definitely starts from the inside and making sure that key decision makers are using the brand and the brand principles to make decisions. As it moves across all the different touch points, it becomes authentic. You arm your community with the tools and words to tell that story consistently over and over and over again, because only when you're telling and proving that brand story over and over does it become real.

# Chapter 13: Stewarding the Brand

Branding is never finished. It has to be continually managed, evolved, and invested in. There are constant changes that are pulling against it, challenging it, threatening it, and trying to replace it, whether that's changes in leadership, political tides, economic ups and downs, or outside interests looking to come in and create their own identity. A brand has to be bigger than all of those things. A brand has to be actively managed. It's definitely not a "set it and forget it" kind of thing. We need to build a strong brand, we need to implement it through daily decisions, but then we need to actively nurture it.

We have to recognize that we are all constantly moving into the future and that the future is always different from our present and our past. It's very natural and very human to want to freeze time and, with it, our places. Many wish we had a time machine and want to take our places back in time to how they were before. But that's not a reality. We are hurtling into the future and therefore will constantly be facing changes, challenges, and new threats. A brand has to navigate all of those challenges and changes.

Thankfully, over the last several years, there has been a change for many organizations that were originally tasked with marketing a destination to shifting their focus to destination management. Many destination marketing organizations (DMOs) are making formal changes to become destination *management* organizations. That can involve a lot of complex, sweeping changes in legislation around funding and taxing as well as organizational restructuring. In most cases, organizations should be making these formal changes, but they don't happen overnight.

The triple bottom line approach to place branding can help any community, whether there's a formal destination marketing or management organization or not, start to evolve into destination management. It allows you to use the brand as a way to think about managing your place, and the triple bottom line forces you to manage and not just market.

Marketing is very focused on the profit component of a triple bottom line, so it is still an important role. That doesn't go away. But as soon as you start to consider the impacts on people in your local community and the impacts of your place, you are now thinking about management as opposed to just marketing alone.

If your community is taking those steps toward having a formal destination management organization, then full speed ahead. Continue doing that, and use the triple bottom line approach to guide your efforts. For those that aren't there yet, don't let the challenge or the funding hurdles keep you from using your brand as a way to manage your place.

If you are only focused on marketing the community and bringing in as many visitors as possible, then something like an amusement park opening up in the middle of your town's only remaining open space could seem like a great idea. It would certainly bring more hotels and more visitors, and your profit would very likely go up. If you consider what building an amusement park in your community would do to the environment, to the land where you would build that amusement park, to the traffic congestion that would come with it, and to the locals that would be displaced or pushed out to make room for hotels and visitor-serving amenities, you will quickly see the problems with bringing an amusement park to your community. That is the value of the triple bottom line approach.

This isn't just for thinking about place management in the context of tourism and visitors, although that's a huge part of it. Overtourism in many destinations is a significant problem that continues to grow. To address overtourism, places are looking at increased visitor fees and taxes. In Europe there have been protests, with locals shooting visitors with water guns and telling them to go back home. Some communities have banned cruises from landing in their towns.

There are many communities that do need visitors, and they are a vital part of their local economy that allows them to have the services and funding they need to thrive. A place brand can absolutely play a role in that. For those communities that are struggling with overtourism, getting the brand right is even more important. We've seen communities with an overtourism problem simply cease all branding efforts. That's the wrong approach. You may need to cease certain marketing efforts, but you actually probably need to double down on branding efforts.

For communities that aren't struggling with overtourism or growth pressures, this is an opportunity to get ahead of that and prevent that from happening, because once you're there, it's much harder to undo that.

I was interviewing a tribal leader in Alaska and talking to her about the role that she felt tourism should play in their community. I remember her saying, "Tourism can be a renewable resource, and I would much rather my child run a tourism-related business than work in the oil fields." Tourism is not a bad thing. It can be a great thing when managed properly because it absolutely can be a renewable resource. It can be additive and not extractive.

Destination management is not just about managing visitors. It is more about reinvesting in our places and managing how our places change and evolve, not just for visitors but for everyone. Funds that come from visitors through hotel taxes and increased sales taxes should not be restricted exclusively to marketing efforts to bring more visitors. It makes zero sense for a place to create rules for itself that do not benefit the community. It can absolutely be a win–win situation, where income gained from visitors can be reinvested into projects and efforts that make things better for the locals and better for the environment and in doing so creates a place that is naturally more attractive to visit. It's a win–win, but right now too many places are handcuffed. They're literally not allowed to use certain funds for anything other than marketing activities.

Thankfully, that's slowly changing. But there are other ways, even before a community makes those formal funding and organizational changes, that they can start to implement true destination management. This starts with collaborative management.

The idea behind collaborative management is recognizing there isn't just one organization, even when you have a DMO, that's tasked with managing a place. Most communities have several organizations and entities that all play different roles and approach managing from different angles but collectively shape the community. There's the city government, the county government, a downtown organization, business groups, cultural groups, tourism, economic development, chambers of commerce, and even large employers like school districts and hospitals. All of these organizations should view themselves as playing a role in destination management, and the key to getting them to do so is getting them in the same room. It's astonishing how many communities have all of these great organizations doing great work that never meet with each other. They are all just off doing their own things. So you first have to get them in the same room together to recognize that despite all of their independent missions, they are all stewards of the same place.

# A *civic* brand is shaped through shared stewardship.

That can start with simply having quarterly meetings that bring all of those different organizations together by getting all of the leaders from those different organizations into a room. In all place-branding projects, those organizations should be actively involved in building the brand, but once you're managing that brand, that work doesn't stop. Those organizations need to continue to come together and continue to meet.

When those organizations meet regularly, they need to talk about the different challenges and projects that they're individually working on and seek ways to collectively help each other while using the brand as a filter in making decisions.

In addition to pulling those different organizations together, a community needs to educate its boards and commissions on the brand and their role in brand management. Whether it's the Public Art Commission, Historic Preservation Commission, or Planning and Zoning Commission, all of those different boards and commissions need to first be involved in building the brand, and they need to be continually educated on the brand as members come on and off the commissions.

Destination management is about stewardship, not ownership. There isn't one group that owns management of the place, and there isn't even one organization that should own the brand. All of these organizations should feel like they have a stake in the brand and have a responsibility to manage it. They should feel like brand champions. We need more champions and fewer gatekeepers.

The brand has to stay front of mind. They need to be continually engaged, trained, and reminded of the brand. Just as we want the community organizations to get together quarterly, we need brand champions to regularly meet with boards and commissions to help them see how the decisions they are making should consider the brand as a decision-making filter.

These are the ways you formally get the brand to start managing the place. You need to get it into those organizations so that the brand seeps into the work they are already doing.

• • •

The next part of brand management is measurement. Measurement is extremely important. It's one of the ways that you justify doing what you're doing. For those that ask or question your value, it's a way to prove you're on the right track and that you're making an impact. However, understanding exactly what to measure and having the resources to actually measure it can be a challenge.

It's easy to get pulled into vanity metrics and numbers that look good and are easy to track or make a nice pie chart. If we go back to the idea that your brand should be that North Star, a reminder of where you're headed, and used in those daily decisions, then I believe we should be more focused on what I call action-based metrics.

These are metrics we can be confident are a result of our efforts and clearly show us if we are taking steps toward our goals. We understand we may not be there yet, and that we may never fully reach our goals, but these show we are continually making progress and taking steps toward where we want to be.

# A *civic* brand proves its value through action.

If you just measure stats that are essentially achieved when you cross a finish line, you can set yourself up for failure. We'd love to measure that and count our successes, but I argue it's more important to measure your steps along the way. We can't just have the end goal be what we're trying to measure. That is the idea behind a brand being a North Star, because the finish line is constantly moving. The goal is to continually strive to head in that direction and course correct when needed. Within a triple bottom line approach, some of the things that we'd love to measure are impacted by so many other factors. A global economic crisis can make things go up or down. So if we just look at pure economic numbers, it can be very hard to tell what role our brand is playing. You can be doing the right things, but those numbers are down because of things outside your control. A place brand can be making progress on environmental issues locally, but no one community is singlehandedly going to stop climate change. Instead, we need to measure those incremental steps toward those big goals. We need to prioritize tracking our progress.

Every place will have its own metrics that make sense, and some will want to track those hard number goals. It should be a mix of metrics specific to your place, your brand principles, and the triple bottom line lens. Let's walk through a couple examples of action-based metrics that we can measure within a triple bottom line approach since those can be universal and apply to every community.

## People

When it comes to a brand's impact on people, one action-based metric you can measure is the number of community engagement events hosted that are connected to the brand. This metric will keep front of mind the continued need for engagement opportunities and events that are focused or driven by brand themes and values and make engagement a culture.

You can measure the number of partnerships formed with those local organizations that we just talked about. You can measure the number of times they meet, the number of organizations involved, the number of decisions they made that were shaped by the brand, and the number of projects they took on. Those are all action-based metrics, and those are all organizations that are impacting the people in your community in many different ways. If the brand plays a role in those organizations getting together and shapes their decisions, the brand impact is now amplified across all of their work.

If your brand has a brand principle like the Hamilton, Ontario, example of being a music city, perhaps you can track how many young musicians participated in a music-related scholarship program that is backed by the brand. When you define your brand goals and brand principles, look for ways to measure their impact on the people in your community.

You can measure the number of times a brand principle or theme was referenced in resident-led or grassroots initiatives. Are residents latching on to the brand and the brand tools? Sometimes it is obvious ways, through design and using tools and templates, but other times it is in more subtle ways through messaging. Are they repeating the message and the core values and referencing the brand indirectly and naturally in their own ways?

## Profit

Profit is probably the easiest one to measure because it's the one that we're used to and is often the only metric category places are measuring. You can certainly measure sales tax, measure the number of visitors and hotel stays, and conduct economic impact studies. There are a lot of different ways to measure profit and prosperity, but I want to focus on some action-based metrics that may be less obvious.

Some action-based ways to measure profit can be the number of businesses that incorporated brand elements or messages into their own marketing. How many are utilizing your made-in brand? Are they using your messaging, graphics, or toolkits in their marketing? Those are good incremental steps. Those are steps that will benefit those individual businesses and their marketing and therefore their profit. If they continue to use them, it means the branding efforts are working and they see value in it.

Running a business will always be a challenge, and in every economy and with every place, there will be businesses that succeed and businesses that fail - in good economies, in bad economies, and in places with a strong place brand and those without one. Those sales numbers and success rates are impacted by so many factors, so they aren't the best metrics to track. A business closing in your downtown could be due to that particular business owner's strategy, personal reasons, industry, or a large number of other reasons. Therefore, tracking the number of businesses opening or closing is not always the best metric, because it's not action based and it's impacted by a wide range of factors.

We can look at talent retention and boomerang residents that move away and come back and engage them to understand what brought them back. In doing so, we can look for signs of brand principles, brand values, messaging, and opportunity created by the brand that show up in their answers. Again, here we'd be looking for mentions of the brand more so than purely counting the number of people.

## Place

In our triple bottom line approach, we're thinking about both place, as in the built environment, as well as the planet, as in the environment. This can often be the hardest to measure because there are so many factors impacting this, but one action-based metric we can measure is the number of new ordinances passed that are aligned with brand goals.

For example, in High Point, North Carolina, we are working with them to implement a placemaking permit to create an ordinance that makes it easier for people to do placemaking initiatives in their community. Their entire brand strategy is centered around the idea that everyone in the community is a creator. So if we make it easier for residents to actively shape their built environment through placemaking, then we are living the brand. When Hamilton, Ontario, legalized busking to align with their music city brand principle, that is absolutely a place metric to measure.

You can measure the number of times brand principles, brand values, and brand messaging find their way into ordinances and decisions that impact the built environment. You can look at the number of people participating in brand-backed sustainability programs, whether it's visitor pledges, sustainability pledges, or the number of people that are engaging with your education materials around environmental impact.

You can measure the number of projects or the square footage of new green space, urban tree canopies, pollinator gardens, and landscaping projects that are due to brand-led placemaking and beautification efforts. If the brand is creating the momentum, the desire, and the need to improve our built environment, then the brand should get credit for those improvements when they come to fruition.

$$\bullet \ \bullet \ \bullet$$

When it comes to managing our places and a place brand, the work is never done. It's constantly evolving, and therefore we need to be constantly learning.

A consistent barrier to progress in cities is the belief that their challenges are solely unique to them. I've heard it a hundred times: "We have a parking problem downtown." "Housing is unaffordable here." "We need to attract more businesses." These are all valid concerns and challenges. But guess what. Nearly every city has the same issues. And if a city *doesn't* have a parking problem, they probably have bigger issues.

This doesn't mean solutions should be wholesale copied and pasted from one city to another, but there is a lot to learn from places that have tackled or are currently wrestling with these issues even if those cities seem very different from yours. Cities don't have to go it alone, yet many approach huge, systemic, and global challenges as if they are the only community facing those problems. Time and time again, when a city is presented with an example from another community, an almost immediate response is "Well, we're not _____."

In consultant interviews, cities often look for experience in their region or with similar-sized places. That's fine, and it's absolutely valuable to have regional context and insight, but there is just as much to learn from cities in completely different contexts. When discussing ideas, people often push back by saying, "Well, we're not Europe," or "We're not New York City." And they're right. They're not. And they don't want to be.

I completely understand that seeing case studies from faraway places can feel irrelevant, even annoying. Every place is unique. The entire point of this book is to help communities uncover their own unique identity. But uniqueness is not an excuse to ignore proven solutions.

What if engineers, doctors, or business owners all said, "Well, that doesn't apply to us," and ignored best practices? Imagine if medical researchers in one country refused to study what worked in another or if aviation experts ignored safer landing techniques because "our airports are different." Progress would stall. Innovation wouldn't happen. Mistakes would be repeated.

Cities are no different. They need to be part of a global learning network. They should be borrowing strategies, experimenting, and adapting, not insulating themselves from solutions because of geography, ideology, or pride. One of the biggest misconceptions is that adopting an idea from another city means becoming like that city. That's just not true.

One of the biggest reasons people reject lessons from other places isn't because those lessons don't apply but because change is hard.

People love their communities, and that love often comes with a deep attachment to how things have always been. Cities, like ecosystems, aren't static. They evolve, whether intentionally or not. The cities that thrive aren't the ones that stubbornly cling to the past or reject outside ideas but are the ones that adapt, borrow, and refine the best strategies to fit their unique context. Change doesn't have to mean losing what makes a place special. It means ensuring it remains a great place to live, now and in the future.

I think Breckenridge, Colorado, is a master class in parking and mobility management and, if examined more closely, offers lessons that towns across the country, especially other mountain towns, could greatly benefit from. However, if mentioned in other slightly less touristy mountain towns, most communities will flat out reject anything associated with Breckenridge, shouting, "Don't Breck us!" as they associate Breckenridge with the challenges of high housing costs, overtourism, and having lost their small mountain town identity.

While it's essential for towns to hold on to what makes them unique, affordable, and special, rejecting ideas simply because they come from a resort town like Breckenridge is a huge mistake. Breckenridge's approach to managing parking, the extensive free bus and shuttle system, the network of neighborhood trail connections and portals, and their prioritization of plowing not just streets but also sidewalks and pedestrian areas are great examples of how towns should approach parking and mobility.

Any negative perceptions one may have with Breckenridge are certainly not the result of its walkability initiatives or parking strategies. Instead, they likely stem from factors unique to Breckenridge's location, like being situated close to I-70 and having a ski resort in the heart of its downtown. If your mountain town doesn't have a ski resort downtown and isn't just down the road from a major interstate, you're probably not going to inherit the same issues just because you study how they manage parking. Those location factors attract a significant influx of visitors, which naturally brings challenges like traffic and congestion. Yes, Breckenridge benefits from generating a lot of revenue to implement its innovative mobility solutions, but that doesn't mean there isn't something to learn. By focusing on what Breckenridge does right, balancing mobility and accessibility with the demands of a bustling destination, other towns can adapt these strategies to their own context without compromising their unique identity.

When it comes to pedestrian and bike infrastructure, if you show someone pictures of Amsterdam, you'll very likely see some eyes roll and hear, "Well, we're not Amsterdam." But many don't realize Amsterdam, like most places, experienced a post-World War II boom in car ownership and urban planning that prioritized automobiles. Streets were widened, neighborhoods were demolished to make way for roads, and cycling and walking infrastructure were neglected. By the late sixties and early seventies, the city faced severe traffic congestion, air pollution, and a growing number of pedestrian and cyclist fatalities.

The turning point came in the 1970s when grassroots movements like the "Stop de Kindermoord" (Stop the Child Murder) campaign highlighted the dangers of car-centric urban planning. Public protests and the 1973 oil crisis led to a shift to policies favoring cycling, walking, and public transit. Over time Amsterdam embraced a more people-centered approach, transforming itself into the cycling haven it is known as today. Many people assume America is too far down the auto-centric path and that Europe, being so old, is just completely different and therefore not relevant, as they don't realize Europe, too, had found themselves in a very auto-dependent state.

While small towns and big urban cities like New York City may seem worlds apart, there are many lessons small towns can learn from large metro areas. Big cities, out of necessity, have been forced to manage challenges that come from high population densities, and these solutions can often be scaled down or adapted to benefit smaller communities.

For example, New York City's public transportation system, though on a much larger scale, highlights the importance of providing alternatives to car dependence. While small towns don't need subways, investing in bike lanes, shared-use paths, or a simple shuttle system can make a huge difference in accessibility and parking challenges. Another lesson is New York's use of public spaces. Parks like the High Line or small pocket parks throughout the city are examples of how underutilized spaces can be transformed into valuable community assets. Small towns often have opportunities to convert empty lots, alleys, or unused spaces into parks, plazas, or markets that foster community connections.

Too often cities resist good ideas because they come from places they think are too different. The reality is that most successful places faced similar challenges before they figured things out. Learning from them doesn't mean giving up your own identity. It means becoming the best version of your city.

In almost every project interview for a comprehensive plan, strategic plan, or master plan I've been part of over the last decade and a half, someone always says, "We don't want a cookie cutter plan." Bingo! That sounds great. It sounds like the right thing to say. After all, who wants to pay for a plan that's just a copy-and-paste job with a few tweaks to the city's name? Nobody.

But the truth is, a lot of cities aren't ready for a highly customized plan, because they haven't tackled the basics yet. What they actually need is a clear, proven approach to address some really foundational and universal elements.

Think of it like hiring a personal trainer. If you're out of shape and just trying to drop a few pounds, you probably don't need a highly customized training plan. You probably just need to eat a little better, walk more, and work out a bit. That's not cookie cutter. It's just what works for everyone. Once you've got the basics down, if you have even higher goals, only then does it makes sense to invest in a more specialized plan. Maybe you want to complete an Ironman or you've got a bad knee or a condition that requires doing a lot more than just the basics. That's when a trainer and highly specialized plan should come in.

It's the same for cities. Every community says they don't want a cookie cutter plan, but the reality is that many plans still end up being just that because what that city needs is the basics. There are things every city should already be doing: maintaining infrastructure, improving walkability, being fiscally responsible and sustainable, and providing basic public services. These aren't cookie cutter ideas. They are the basics. If your city isn't doing the basics, don't waste time pretending you need a custom plan to figure it out.

The real problem is when cities blow their budget and time on elaborate planning processes that only end up telling them what everyone already knew. They get so caught up in not being cookie cutter that they waste resources on the obvious stuff, and by the time they get to the parts of the plan that actually need customization, there's no budget left to actually do any of it.

Cities need to be honest about where they are. If you're not doing the basics, embrace a simple, straightforward plan to fix that first. Once you've caught up, then you can invest in the custom work that will take your community to the next level. There is a lot you can learn from other communities' plans that would directly apply to you. Look at those plans. Look at what other cities are doing. Look at their parking plans. Look at their trail networks and connections. I bet there is a lot there that applies to you but most cities ignore because they feel their town is too unique.

A similar thing happens not just when other places are used as examples but even certain words are used. Word choice matters. Words can be weaponized and polarizing, and it's unfortunate when that gets in the way of places becoming the best version of themselves. If the word "urban," "density," or even "equity" is used in certain communities, whatever follows will be rejected.

The terms "urban" and "density" are often misunderstood, which can lead to pushback and flat-out rejection in community planning. "Urban" simply refers to the built environment of buildings, streets, and public spaces and is as relevant to small rural towns as it is to a large city. Similarly, "density" is simply a measure of development and a tool that can address important issues like land use, housing affordability, aging in place, and preserving open spaces and natural amenities.

Unfortunately, these terms are often interpreted through a political or ideological lens and are mischaracterized as signaling progressive agendas, causing people to assume the intent is to turn their small, rural town into a big city. This can lead to fear and rejection of ideas that could genuinely benefit the community and, in many cases, could actually help them maintain what they love about their community.

For consultants and city leaders, it is important to be mindful of these perceptions and to choose words carefully. Avoid polarizing terms where possible, and instead use language that resonates with the community. For example, rather than saying "urban form," consider referring to "the built environment." Instead of "density," talk about "efficient land use" or "compact development," or explain how diverse housing types allow residents to age in place when discussing zoning.

At the same time, education should be a key part of engagement and communication. Consultants should take the opportunity to clarify what these terms really mean and explain their applications in ways that are relevant to that community. Rather than focusing on technical definitions, demonstrate how higher-density housing options can allow local seniors to downsize without leaving the community or protect cherished natural areas by concentrating development. You can do that without even saying those words. By combining careful word choice with a focus on education, we can help communities move past the drama and start solving problems.

Many communities insist their challenges are unique, but if they simply studied what other places have done, they'd see that many of the solutions they need are already out there. Instead of dismissing examples, ask, "What aspects of this could work for us? How can we adapt this to fit our context? What mistakes can we avoid by learning from others?"

No place is exactly like yours. Cities that embrace learning from anywhere and everywhere are the ones that truly thrive. Our places need to continue to learn from other places, just as we all need to learn from other people.

In summary, a place brand viewed through the triple bottom

line lens is absolutely the best way to evolve into destination management and turn a place brand into a true *civic* brand. We have to get collaborative and invite all the different organizations and players in so that the entire community is managing the place through aligned actions. We need to measure our progress and impact through action-based metrics and continue to learn from other places because the work of place branding is never done.

## Chapter 14: It Starts With You

Reflecting on the wide range of places and people we've had the privilege to work with, every project started because someone in that community recognized that their place had more to offer and wasn't reaching its full potential. They recognized the challenges in their community, but they also saw the opportunity. They put their trust in us to help them tackle those challenges, tell their story, and build a better future for their community.

Just as a street is a collection of homes and businesses, a city is a collection of neighborhoods, and a country is a collection of cities and states, our planet is a collection of individual places. For the time being, this is the only planet we have. Your country is the country you have, your city is the city you have, and this is the neighborhood you have.

We need to recognize the power of place in shaping everything about our lives. Once we recognize how important our places are, we need to become hypervigilant and ensure that we have a shared vision and drive to manage and nurture our places.

We need to recognize that a place brand, when done right, can be the tip of the spear that can lead everything else. It guides our planning decisions, our investments, our budgets, our priorities, our pride, and our stewardship. The place brand pulls it all together. It influences and filters down into every decision and drives us forward.

We need to expand the understanding and role of place branding and recognize that it isn't just about marketing. It isn't just about messaging and communications. It's about making all of our places better. It's about making every place the best version of itself so that our places are more equitable, more sustainable, and more resilient for future generations.

We need to recognize that if a brand is our North Star, then we need to hold it accountable, and the triple bottom line approach of people, profit, and place gives us the framework to do that and make sure that we are focused on the right things.

So my call to action for everyone is to embrace that responsibility of shaping and stewarding your place. Be a leader and the change that your place needs and deserves. Recognize that it's our small, collective daily actions that collectively build the future and shape our places.

# ACKNOWLEDGEMENTS

To Banner, none of this would be possible without you. From dreaming up this company eighteen years ago together, to countless brainstorming sessions, to encouraging me when I doubt myself, and to picking up an immense amount of slack when I was traveling for projects or writing this book, you've been my partner in every way. Not a word of this book exists without you, and there would be no reason to write it without you. Plus, there would be a lot more typos!

To my boys, Andrew and Charlie, I am endlessly proud of the young men you've become. Your character and kindness give me hope. The work of creating better places is slow and challenging, but it's worth every moment because it's for you, your generation, and those that follow. I know your generation will care for our places better than any before, and I am excited to watch you lead.

To my mom, Lynda Short, thank you for dedicating your life to providing me with everything I needed and more. You've always been an inspiration not just for the opportunities you've created for me, but in the countless lives you've shaped through your lifelong career of teaching and caring for others.

To my in-laws, Dana and David Winans, thank you for raising such an incredible daughter and for being a model of how business and family can not only coexist, but make each other stronger.

To the entire CivicBrand team, this book is a reflection of the work we've done together. Brisa Byford, thank you for being a true creative partner. Many of the ideas in this book have been shaped through years of our collaboration and conversations. Colin

Coolidge, your work ethic and dedication are a continued inspiration and the backbone of building CivicBrand. Kelsy Boyle, your fresh perspective, creative talent, and deep passion for place makes everything you touch better. To Matt Henry and Clay Hervey, your talents in visual storytelling have brought so many of our projects to life in powerful ways, making our impact even greater. Layne Ferguson, Landon Ferguson, and Connor Cox, thank you for your expertise and helping us reimagine how brands can live in the built environment. To Kinsey Stewart, Shiloe du Vall, Jeremy Monroe, Benjamin Steiner, Nic Pfost, and the extended CivicBrand family - your creativity and energy have helped take CivicBrand to the next level at each step along this journey.

To all of our clients, thank you for trusting us. It takes courage to take ownership of your story and lead your community with clarity and intention, and it is an honor to work alongside you.

To my many partners and collaborators, thank you for helping move this work forward in so many ways. In nearly two decades of work, it's impossible to thank everyone who has helped shape this work.

Chuck Marohn, your work has had a profound influence on me. Your belief in this book and your generous contribution of the foreword mean more than you will ever know. Thank you for your leadership and clarity that this industry desperately needs.

To the Proud Places crew - Jeff Siegler, Bernice Radle, Phil Eich, Ben Muldrow, Jaime Izurieta, Joe Borgstrom, and Jenifer Acosta - your friendship, talent, and passion inspire me constantly. You are each doing important work, and I'm proud to be part of this community with you.

Jamie Sabbach, thank you for raising the bar across civic leadership. Your deep expertise and commitment to education are an inspiration, and I greatly value our partnership and friendship.

Torr Leonard, thank you for being a one-person internet and idea machine. Your shared links, insights, and humor have shaped more of my thinking than I care to admit.

Brad Moulton, thank you for being a lifelong friend, collaborator, and a key reason that CivicBrand exists.

Finally, a few people who helped make this book happen in a very direct way. Joe Stone, thank you for being an early reader, a trusted voice, and for all you do in our community. Travis Volz, thank you for your help in spreading the word about this project. To Jonathon Stalls, your art and advocacy were a steady source of inspiration. Thank you for your encouragement and the generous advice you offered as an experienced author.

# WORKS CITED

**Books:**

Barger Jr., Jim, and Dr. Carlton Hicks. Jimmy Carter: Rivers & Dreams. Athens, GA: Bitter Southerner/BS Publishing, 2024.

Chouinard, Yvon, and Vincent Stanley. The Responsible Company: What We've Learned from Patagonia's First 40 Years. Patagonia, 2012.

Elkington, John. Cannibals with Forks: The Triple Bottom Line of 21st Century Business. Capstone, 1997.

Jacobs, Jane. The Death and Life of Great American Cities. New York: Random House, 1961.

Marohn, Charles. Strong Towns: A Bottom-Up Revolution to Rebuild American Prosperity. Hoboken, NJ: Wiley, 2019.

Montgomery, Charles. Happy City: Transforming Our Lives Through Urban Design. New York: Farrar, Straus and Giroux, 2013.

Norman, Don. The Design of Everyday Things. New York: Basic Books, 2013.

Sussman, Ann, and Justin B. Hollander. Cognitive Architecture: Designing for How We Respond to the Built Environment. New York: Routledge, 2015.

**Articles and Reports:**

Chayka, Kyle. "Welcome to Airspace: How the Coolest Places on Earth Got Blended into One." The Verge, August 3, 2016.

Murthy, Vivek H. "My Parting Prescription for America." Washington, D.C.: U.S. Department of Health & Human Services, 2022.

World Bank. "'Crowding In' Effect of Public Investment on Private Investment Revisited." Washington, D.C.: World Bank, 2023.

**Film / Documentary:**

Buy Now! The Shopping Conspiracy. Directed by Nic Stacey. Netflix, 2024. Streaming video.

# ABOUT THE AUTHOR

Ryan Short is the co-founder of CivicBrand, a place-branding consultancy he started with his wife, Banner Short. Since 2008, they have helped lead engagement-driven branding, placemaking, and destination management and marketing projects across the United States, guiding communities toward becoming more vibrant, equitable, and loveable places.

He has been published on Forbes.com and is a regular speaker at national and international conferences on place branding, civic engagement, and economic development. He is also the host of *Eyes On The Street,* a podcast that explores the intersection of community, culture, and design through conversations with civic leaders and changemakers.

Ryan lives in Salida, Colorado, with Banner and their two sons. When he's not working, he enjoys fly fishing, live music, and spending time with his family.

·

www.ingramcontent.com/pod-product-compliance
Lightning Source LLC
Chambersburg PA
CBHW030506210326
41597CB00013B/816